THE ART AND CRAFT OF POETRY

Borgo Press Books by Michael R. Collings

All Calm, All Bright: Christmas Offerings
The Art and Craft of Poetry: Twenty Exercises Toward Mastery
Brian Aldiss
Dark Transformations: Deadly Visions of Change
The Films of Stephen King
GemLore: An Introduction to Precious and Semi-Precious Gemstones
The House Beyond the Hill: A Novel of Horror
The Many Facets of Stephen King
Naked to the Sun: Dark Visions of Apocalypse
Piers Anthony
Scaring Us to Death: The Impact of Stephen King on Popular Culture
Singer of Lies: A Novel of Fantasy
Wordsmith, Part One: The Veil of Heaven: A Science Fantasy Novel
Wordsmith, Part Two: The Thousand Eyes of Flame: A Science Fantasy Novel

THE ART AND CRAFT OF POETRY

TWENTY EXERCISES TOWARD MASTERY

Second Edition, Revised and Expanded

by

Michael R. Collings

Emeritus Professor of English
Seaver College
Pepperdine University

THE BORGO PRESS

An Imprint of Wildside Press LLC

MMIX

Borgo Literary Guides
ISSN 0891-9623

Number Nine

Copyright © 1996, 2009 by Michael R. Collings

All poetry remains the property of the individual poets

All rights reserved.
No part of this book may be reproduced in any form
without the expressed written consent
of the author and publisher.
Printed in the United States of America

I am particularly grateful to W. Gregory Stewart, a fine poet—both artist and craftsman—for his permission to reprint "Robo Ben" and "Dædalus" and for his support of the Pepperdine University Creative Writing program and its arts magazine, *Expressionists*.

www.wildsidepress.com

SECOND EDITION

Contents

Foreword 9

Some Preliminary Matters—What is Poetry? 13
    Characteristics of a Poem 13
    Simple Vs. Sophisticated Poetry 14
    Lineation 23
Emotion and Intellect in Poetry 29
Exercises 33
    1. Repetition 33
    2. Sources of Poetry—Visual Triggers 41
    3. Sources of Poetry—Myth and Literature 44
    4. Cinquain 50
        Bonus Exercise: Haiku 53
    5. Fibonacci Sequence 55
Meter 60
Exercises 69
    6. Theodore Roethke Imitation 69
        Bonus Exercise: Herrick Imitation 73
    7. Revision I 74
        Bonus Exercise 76
    8. Metrical Imitations 78
        Bonus Exercise 84
        Bonus Exercise 86
    9. Gwendolyn Brooks Exercise 88
Compression I: Saying Much with Little 90
Exercises 95
    10. Metrical Verse 95
        Bonus Exercise: Non-traditional Sonnet 101

11. Revision II	103
12. Villanelle	108
13. Sestina	113
Free Verse	121
14. Free Verse—Object	123
15. Free Verse—Three Subjects	128
16. Free Verse—Three Themes	136
17. Free Verse—W. Gregory Stewart Imitation	144
Compression II: Eliminating Unnecessary Articles	149
18. Concrete Poem	157
Bonus Exercise: Cento	160
19. Parody/Pastiche	162
Compression III: Linking Verbs	170
20. Revision III	175
Personal Poetry Inventory	183
About the Author	187

The Art and Craft of Poetry

Foreword

While many of the poems referred to as models have been posted on internet sites, some exercises in this sequence are keyed to materials in the following books, although it is not necessary to purchase them in order to explore the possibilities of poetry presented here:

Drury, John. *The Poetry Dictionary.* Cincinnati OH: Story Press, 1995. [Drury]. Drury is particularly valuable for its detailed discussions of literary forms and movements. The sections need not be read in sequence.

Rosengarten, Herbert, and Amanda Goldrick-Jones, eds. *The Broadview Anthology of Poetry.* Peterborough, Ontario, Canada; Orchard Park NY, 1993. [*TBAP*]. The *Broadview Anthology* provides access to poetry from Chaucer to the present, many of which will form the kernel of discussion; at the same time, the anthology allows students to explore professional-level writing.

Several additional texts are highly recommended for any writers, primarily as adjuncts to the writing process:

Hodges, John C. and Mary E. Whitten. *Harbrace College Handbook.* Current edition. Poets frequently defy the conventions of language, re-defining the functions of punctuation marks, grammatical structures, etc., for poetic purposes. However, in almost every case, the poets in question fully understand the conventions *before* altering them. Effective poetry must convince their readers that, in spite of experimental surfaces, the poets understand the underpinnings of English grammar and usage.

Collegiate Dictionary, such as *The American Heritage Dictionary*. Current edition. The same caveat holds for spelling: contemporary poetry often re-works and reforms words, but before poets do that they must be familiar with the standards they are rejecting. Effective poems must convince their readers that any aberrant forms are purposeful rather than accidental or stemming from ignorance.

The accompanying exercises are designed primarily for writers already acquainted with the rudiments of poetry: meter, rhythm, rhyme, figures, images, etc. While several pages are devoted to definitions and discussions, most of *The Art and Craft of Poetry* concentrates on exercises and, most frequently, college students' responses to those exercises.

Most of the poems included as examples come from students in intermediate Creative Writing classes over the past twenty years. These poems and others like them formed the basis of discussion in classes spanning over fifteen years.

NOTE: Many of the student poems—here reproduced as originally submitted, without the benefit of subsequent revising—are unusually well done; others demonstrate common weaknesses, and close readings may suggest serious problems as well as ways other writers might avoid those dangers. All, however, show a commitment to writing, to poetry, and to art. They are included to demonstrate individual responses to poetry; as student works or works-in-progress, they are intended to provide models for discussion. You are encouraged to read them, assess their effectiveness as poetry for you, and emulate the strengths you find in them.

I am particularly grateful to the following former students for allowing me to incorporate their voices into this handbook: Janna Anderson, Lisa Bates, Carter Boisvert, Joanie Chan, Ethan Collings, Ty de Long, Alex Duncan, Robert Efford, Allison Elms, Christian Hawkey, Erin Kayler, Kim Kooyers, Marnee Lewis, Mercedes Martinez, Adrienne Maxwell, Tamar Moore, Rachel Moreno, Matt Oden, Nichole Paré, Alan Regan, Keith Skilling, Michael Strickland, Amy Vicker, Jason Wall, Chad Weiss, and

John Weseley. Without their dedication as students and writers, this handbook would not have been possible.

—Michael R. Collings
Meridian, Idaho
March 2009

The Art and Craft of Poetry:

Twenty Exercises Towards Mastery

Some Preliminary Matters—What is Poetry?

C. S. Lewis argues that before we can judge the merits of anything—from a cathedral to a poem—we must first understand what it is. Similarly, before tackling the issue of writing poetry, we must first understand what a poem is ... and what it is not.

Characteristics of a Poem

Most theorists of poetry generally identify four basic characteristics of poetry:

- Lineation—often considered the only absolute differentia between prose and poetry, although some theorists argue even this point. In most poetry, however, the poet retains absolute control over line length and division.

- Sound/Music—the effects of rhyme, repetitions of various sorts, and the effects produced by specific word combinations.

- Rhythm—recurrent patterns of sound, pitch, stress, accent, etc., including both formal metrics and less formal repetitive syntactical, grammatical, and thematic patterns.

- Compression—the art of folding into the poem more meaning than a literal reading produces; this might include not only removing linguistic deadwood but also strengthening image and symbol.

SIMPLE VS. SOPHISTICATED POETRY:

"To a biologist, simple forms of life are *simple* and complex forms are *sophisticated.* Thus, the bird is not *better* in any objective sense than the jellyfish, but it is far more sophisticated in that the potential of living matter has been developed much further.

"As an individual, the biologist may prefer a canary to a jellyfish as a pet or may feel that the jellyfish is *better* as an example of living tissue; but acting as a biologist, his or her use of the terms *simple* and *sophisticated* is objective.

"Does all poetry have to be sophisticated? Of course not. Judging by the verse of greeting cards, far more people prefer their poetry simple—regular meter, conventional sentiments, and the cozy familiarity of time-tested clichés. Writing simple verse is a craft and there are books that teach it. But this is not one.

"Sophisticated literature is the subject of this text. It is by definition complex, but it is not necessarily cluttered or obscure. A fly's eye, for example, is in some ways more complex in structure than a human eye, but as an instrument of sight it is far from sophisticated. It cannot see as well. In the same way, a villanelle with its complex systems of rhymes and repeated lines is structurally more complicated than, say, a three-line haiku; but in some cases the haiku is more sophisticated because it *does* more—it has a wider, more subtle range of suggestion." (Stephen Minot, *Three Genres*)

Discussion: To what extent are the following poems "simple"? Is one more "sophisticated" than the other? If so, what elements contribute to its increased depth and complexity? Is there a specific moment in each when the poem begins to falter *as poem*? Remember, "simple" and "sophisticated" in this context merely *describe*; they do not *judge*.

Joyce Kilmer, TREES

I think that I shall never see
A poem lovely as a tree.
A tree whose hungry mouth is pressed

Against the earth's sweet flowing breast;
A tree that looks to God all day
And lifts her leafy arms to pray;
A tree that may in summer wear
A nest of robins in her hair;
Upon whose bosom snow has lain;
Who intimately lives with rain.
Poems are made by fools like me,
But only God can make a tree.

Anonymous greeting-card verses:

> The real Christmas feeling
> That warm friendly glow
> Comes from greeting the people
> We're happy to know.

> May the beautiful
> blessings of Christmas
> With its message
> of hope and cheer
> Be for you a joyous reminder
> That our Savior
> is with you all year.

FOR FURTHER DISCUSSION:
Ezra Pound, "In a Station of the Metro"

EXERCISE: Compare the poems in the following sets in terms of simplicity or sophistication. In each set, one of the poems will be blunter, more direct; one will makes its point less directly, through image, metaphor, and structure:

SET I:

A POISON TREE

I was angry with my friend:
I told my wrath, my wrath did end.
I was angry with my foe:
I told it not, my wrath did grow.

And I watered it in fears,
Night and morning with my tears;
And I sunnéd it with smiles,
And with soft deceitful wiles.

And it grew both day and night
Till it bore an apple bright;
And my foe beheld it shine,
And he knew that it was mine,

And into my garden stole
When the night had veiled the pole:
In the morning glad I see
My foe stretched out beneath the tree.

TEACH ME TO LIVE

Teach me to live! 'tis easier far to die;
   Gently and silently to pass away,
On earth's long night to close the heavy eye,
   And waken in the realms of glorious day.

Teach me that harder lesson, how to live,
   To *serve Thee* in the *darkest paths of life;*
Arm me for conflict now; fresh vigor give,
   And make me more than conqueror in the strife.

Teach me to live! my daily cross to bear,
   Nor murmur though I bend beneath its load.

Only be with me; *let me feel Thee near;*
   Thy smile sheds gladness on the darkest road.

Teach me to live, and find my life in Thee;
   Looking from earth and earthly things away;
Let me not falter, but untiringly
Press on, and gain new strength and power each day.

Teach me to live! with kindly words for all;
   Wearing no cold, repulsive brow of gloom;
Waiting with cheerful patience, till Thy call
   Summon my spirit to her heavenly home.

SET II:

GOD'S PLANS

Sometime, when all life's lessons have been learned,
   And sun and stars forever more have set,
The things which our weak judgment here have spurned,
   The things o'er which we grieved with lashes wet,
Will flash before us out of life's dark night,
   As stars shine most in deeper tints of blue:
And we shall see how all God's plans were right,
   And how what seemed reproof was love most true.

And we shall see, while we frown and sigh,
   God's plans go on as best for you and me;
How, when called, he heeded not our cry,
   Because his wisdom to the end could see.
And e'en as prudent parents disallow
   Too much of sweet to craving boyhood,
So God, perhaps, is keeping from us now
   Life's sweetest things because it seemeth good.

And if, sometimes, commingling with life's wine,
   We find the wormwood and rebel and sink,

Be sure a wiser hand than yours or mine
    Pours out this potion for our lips to drink.
And if some friend we love is living low,
    Where human kisses cannot reach his face,
Oh, do not blame the loving Father so,
    But bear your sorrow with obedient grace!

And you shall shortly know that lengthened breath
    Is not the sweetest gift God sends his friends,
And that, sometimes, the sable pall of death
    Conceals the fairest bloom his love can send.
If we could push ajar the gates of life,
    And stand within and all God's workings see,
We could interpret all this doubt and strife,
    And for each mystery could find a key.

But not to-day. Then be content, poor heart;
    God's plans, like lilies pure and white, unfold.
We must not tear the close shut leaves apart—
    Time will reveal the calyxes of gold.
And if, through patient toil we reach the land,
    Where tired feet, with sandals loose, may rest,
When we shall clearly know and understand,
    I think we will say that "God knows best."

PIED BEAUTY

  Glory be to God for dappled things—
    For skies of couple-color as a brinded cow,
      For rose-moles all in stipple upon trout that swim;
  Fresh-firecoal chestnut-falls; finches' wings;
    Landscape plotted and pieced—fold, fallow and plow;
      And all their trades, their gear and tackle and trim.

  All things counter, original, spare, strange;
    Whatever is fickle, freckled (who knows how?)
      With swift, slow; sweet, sour; adazzle, dim;

He fathers-forth whose beauty is past change:
   Praise him.

SET III:

THE TOYS

My little Son, who looked from thoughtful eyes
And moved and spoke in quiet grown-up wise,
Having my law the seventh time disobeyed,
I struck him, and dismissed
With hard words and unkissed,
His Mother, who was patient, being dead.
Then, fearing lest his grief should hinder sleep,
I visited his bed,
But found him slumbering deep,
With darkened eyelids, and their lashes yet
From his late sobbing wet.
And I, with moan,
Kissing away his tears, left others of my own;
For on a table drawn beside his head,
He had put, within his reach,
A box of counters and a red-veined stone,
A piece of glass abraded by the beach,
And six or seven shells,
A bottle with bluebells,
And two French copper coins, ranged there with careful art,
To comfort his sad heart.
So when that night I prayed
To God, I wept, and said:
Ah, when at last we lie with trancéd breath,
Not vexing Thee in death,
And thou rememberest of what toys
We made our joys,
How weakly understood
Thy great commanded good,
Then, fatherly not less

Than I whom Thou has moulded from the clay,
Thou'lt leave Thy wrath, and say,
"I will be sorry for their childishness."

IS THERE ROOM IN ANGEL LAND?

> "These lines were written after hearing the following touching incident related by a minister. A mother, who was preparing some flour to bake into bread, left it for a moment, when little Mary, with childish curiosity to see what it was, took hold of the dish, when it fell to the floor, spilling the contents. The mother struck the child a severe blow, saying, with anger, that she was always in the way. Two weeks after, little Mary sickened and died. On her death-bed, while delirious, she asked her mother if there would be room for her among the angels. 'I was always in your way, mother; you had no room for little Mary! And will I be in the angels' way? Will they have no room for me?' The broken-hearted mother then felt no sacrifice would be too great, could she have saved her child."

Is there room among the angels
   For the spirit of your child?
Will they take your little Mary
   In their loving arms so mild?
Will they ever love me fondly,
   As my story-books have said?
Will they find a home for Mary—
   Mary, numbered with the dead?
Tell me truly, darling mother!
   Is there room for such as me?
Will I gain the home of spirits,
   And the shining angels see?

I have sorely tried you, mother,
   Been to you a constant care,
And you will not miss me, mother,

When I dwell among the fair;
For you have no room for Mary;
   She was ever in your way;
And fears the good will shun her!
   Will they, darling mother, say?
Tell me—tell me truly—mother,
   Ere life's closing hour doth come,
Do you think that they will keep me
   In the shining angels' home?

I was not so wayward, mother,
   Nor so very—very bad,
But that tender love would nourish,
   And make Mary's heart so glad!
Oh! I yearned for pure affection,
   In this world of bitter woe;
And I long for bliss immortal,
   In the land where I must go!
Tell me once again, dear mother,
   Ere you take the parting kiss,
Will the angels bid me welcome,
   To that land of perfect bliss?

LITTLE BOY BLUE

The little toy dog is covered with dust,
   But sturdy and staunch he stands;
And the little toy soldier is red with rust,
   And his musket moulds in his hands.
Time was when the little toy dog was new,
   And the soldier was passing fair;
And that was the time when our Little Boy Blue
   Kissed them and put them there.

"Now, don't you go till I come," he said,
   "And don't you make any noise!"
So, toddling off to his trundle-bed,

He dreamt of the pretty toys;
And, as he was dreaming, an angel song
　　Awakened our Little Boy Blue—
Oh! the years are many, the years are long,
　　But the little toy friends are True!

Ay, faithful to Little Boy Blue they stand,
　　Each in the same old place—
Awaiting the touch of a little hand,
　　The smile of a little face;
And they wonder as waiting the long years through
　　In the dust of the little chair,
What has become of our Little Boy Blue
　　Since he kissed them and put them there.

LINEATION

Lineation refers to choice of line length, a technique essential to much modern poetry, which often relies heavily on placement on the page, length of lines, and physical presentation. Compare, for example, poetry by Walt Whitman, Marianne Moore, and Allen Ginsberg, with their long lines and biblical cadences that sweep majestically from margin to margin; poems such as Susan Musgrave's "Lure" (*TBAP* 882) or William Carlos Williams' "The Red Wheelbarrow" and "This Is Just To Say," which often seem to hug the left-hand margin of the page; and poems by Lawrence Ferlinghetti, Judith Rodriguez, and others which seem scattered almost at random, with lines punctuating expanses of white space.

The poet's choice of form often dictates basic line length, however, particularly in traditional metrical forms. Note the different effects in the following poems:

M

                i

A thousand wives lie close to heart,

intimáte,
shape shivering breasts to word-dream

couplings,
bald lips to   consummation
in the lust
                            of vividry
and *elán vital* of transmutation
pressing painful birth into a wilder universe
part and part and part and intimation
timbreling into
                        completion

ii

A thousand secret selves clamor
for carved ears,
a thousand altérnate selves,

elementals recording what is/seems and was
and what may be—
a thousand pale prospective nightmares

                    dreams
expulsive energies define
and
redefine into infinity

iii

A thousand deaths thrive here
a thousand
                    apparitional
cheddar-scaled goldfish
floating in blue tepid water and

                    cannibalizing
bloated skull and unzipped spine
of one that once was of their own kind
when it still lived—
                    but failed
transmutation
                    became
consummation
rocking on aquarial blue-plastic coated stones

iv

A thousand children sleep soundly
in typic beds—

progeny of imagery,

                            heirs of rhythms

potentialities
unenfleshed and ripening
                    tattering on weak
iambs
                    to dream
mortality
and pungent smells
of
swollen ripeness
                    pressed
in black arc-lines
against a thousand
stained sheets

STRINGING BUTTONS

Stringing buttons—hunched on the worn pine floor,
   Its planks velvet smooth from half-century
Of hands scrubbing, polishing—musty air
   Warm with subtle gossip, whispered words we

Youngsters ignored.... We strung buttons on hanks
   Of time-grayed cotton-thread and squabbled for
Favorites: foil-backed glass; glossy jet, ink-
   Black-deep; mock turquoise; hand-cut bone, smooth, clear—

While hour on hour grandmothers stitched staid quilts,
   Wove intricate lines with white cotton strands
Through patterns pieced from scraps—old aprons, shirts
   Sunday dresses faded and worn breath-thin;

Our cotton threads coiled in the button box—
We never cared that none had end-thread knots.

VULTURE

Or perhaps vulture
(as my son avers

although he reclined
half-sleeping when

the black shadow
rose, soused

as if to clutch
with careful claw

my small Ford,
and disappeared

above the tunnel's
mouth)—flash

of red-on-black
glint of hooked

beak but mostly
bulk and blackly

ominous shade
whispers death

and rises as I pass
into darkness

DISCUSSION QUESTIONS:
1. What principles govern lineation in each poem? How effective are those principles in light of the final poem?
2. In which poem does the poet more fully seem to control where and/or when lines begin and end?

3. Is the chosen form appropriate for each poem?

Line length intensifies poetic effects in many ways. Compare the following passages:

> Freedom of the mind requires not only, or not even especially, the absence of legal constraints but the presence of alternative thoughts.

> Just to say thank you to the one who laid a pair of pruning shears open on my driveway yesterday; I shall use them on the roses and save my four new tires.

Is there anything particularly "poetic" about either (excepting for the moment the homage to William Carlos Williams implicit in the second)? Which of the two sounds less like poetry, more like prose?
When the lines break into meaningful sub-units—poetic "lines"—the impact of each becomes more apparent. Even a prose passage can attain to something like poetic emphasis:

FREEDOM OF THE MIND
                requires
not only,
   or not even especially,
  the absence
    of legal constraints

but

the presence
      of alternative thoughts.

                      — "quoted" from Allan Bloom,
                      The Closing of the American Mind

JUST TO SAY

thank you
to
the one

who laid a pair
of pruning
shears

open on
my driveway
yesterday;

I shall use
them
on the roses

and save
my four
new tires.

DISCUSSION: Which seems more effective as poetry? How else could the original passages be divided to create "poetry"?

Emotion and Intellect in Poetry

For a few pages, I would like to re-don my professorial cap (you know, the square one with the tassel) and posit two poles from which poetry may start: emotion and intellect. There are, of course, many other ways to discuss poetics, but these two seem at the moment most relevant. But before the discussion, two assertions:

Neither approach is right.

Neither approach is wrong.

Most poetry would in fact fit nicely on a continuum between extremes, and it is perhaps impossible to write a piece that emanates exclusively from one or the other. But for the purposes of discussion, let's begin there.

Poetry of Emotion draws most strongly, obviously, from the depths of the poet's emotions: love, fear, loneliness, hatred. Such poetry has as a primary intention recreating that emotion, in many cases privately and personally; readers become in essence adjuncts to the process, at times even irrelevant to it. The poem is directed inward, to the poet's core. It becomes a means of emotional adjustment, a way to extract a particular emotional state and express it directly.

Such poetry relies little on poetic conventions and greatly on experience. The poet speaks directly, often in first person, often alluding to private experiences readers are neither expected nor invited to share. In some instances, a specific, single reader might serve as audience—particularly in poems of love or loss—but more commonly even that reader is peripheral to the expression of deep and often painful emotion.

Such basics of written communication as grammar, syntax, spelling, punctuation, and sentence structure rank low on the poet's scale of priorities, sometimes even perceived as hindering the 'honest' expression of emotion. Revision becomes antithetical to the purposes of the poem; to hold the poem up to scrutiny, to alter its white-hot rhythms and diction would be to diminish the authenticity of its emotional content. Such poeticisms as image, simile, metaphor, or symbol occur only tangentially, as it were, as by-products of the poet's need to allow the emotion to surface.

POETRY OF INTELLECT, on the other hand, relies, equally obviously, on intellect; not on reason or rationality, per se, but on the conscious manipulation of them. The poem becomes a puzzle to create and to interpret. The poet becomes distanced in the sense that words become means to an end, tools by which to create a preconceived artifact.

Poetic conventions become the driving force behind the construct. Image and simile may occur, but more usually the more rigidly logical, objective tropes predominate: metaphor, with its conscious awareness and manipulation of similarities and differences between unexpectedly juxtaposed objects; and symbol, with its equal if not greater requirement of cerebral engagement to state effectively an idea not in fact present in the poem.

Such poems exploit the possibilities of form to the utmost, either traditional forms, including requirements of meter and rhyme, word or syllable count; or nonce forms in which free-verse lines express preconceived structures. Language similarly becomes a tool for puzzle-making and -solving, with acrostics, anagrams, palindromes, and other related techniques at times subordinating sense and meaning.

Again, I'm considering here extreme polarities possible in poetry. Most, if not all poetry, lies on the continuum between extremes; and much of the greatest poetry clusters near the center.

However, there is a point to be made by discussing these polarities. Much of the apparent discord that arise between poets and respondents, between poets and poets, may result from individuals not differentiating between two essentially antithetical purposes for writing.

I tend toward intellectual poetry, for example; it bothers me, and for me detracts substantially from a poem's effectiveness, to see misspellings, grammatical infelicities, awkward or strained syntax (particularly in service of an equally awkward or strained rhyme).

Form frequently seems preferable to free verse, since it automatically creates an intellectual challenge that I appreciate—how to communicate specific ideas, images, and, yes, even emotions, within the constraints of pre-existing line or stanzaic expectations. At the same time it provides relatively objective criteria for assessing poems: how well do they perform within those expectations. My own work tends to be formal…and at times it tends to be dispassionate, distanced, cold.

ON POETRY AS A FAÇADE BEHIND WHICH THE ESSENCE LURKS

> Meter comes easily. English tends to
> Shift and swirl in rhythmic fall-then-rise.
> Syllables allow themselves (almost) no
> Hesitance. Sounds link in subtle ways
> But can be tracked and traced across crisp lines,
> Arrows drawn if needed to make clear
> How "m" persists, or "l," what strengths it gains
> By repetition. What remains to mar
> The texture of a piece, to hinder
> Transformation from mere craft to art
> (If one can hope for such in fonder
> Thoughts) is that oblique, intrinsic part,
> That revelatory, quintessential goal:
> The power and the passion and the soul.

Others poets, however, equally if not more proficient and imaginative poets, tend toward emotional poetry. For them free verse is often preferable to form since it allows for, if not invites openly, overt expression of emotion. Niceties of grammatical conventions can be overlooked in favor of intensity, authenticity, excitement, and directness. Evaluating such poems becomes itself an act of emotion, of subjectivity: Do I like this poem? At the most distant extreme, that question might frequently supersede a more difficult question: Why do I like this poem?

There may be, as noted in the beginning of this consideration, many other ways to discuss poetry. But regardless of other options, it may be helpful to keep a couple of questions in mind when we approach a poem. What does the poet's choice to write a sonnet, or a haiku, or meter and rhyme, or stripped-down free-verse suggest about why the poet wrote this particular poem? And what can we therefore legitimately expect to encounter when we enter it? Taking a moment to identify a poem as essentially emotion-oriented or intellect-oriented may make the experience of reading poems more beneficial, more constructive, and ultimately more enjoyable.

EXERCISES

1. REPETITION
Write at least fifteen lines, each beginning with the same word or phrase: "I wish," "Once," "Then," etc. Write without stopping or using conscious structures or ideas. Generate a series of lines with ideas and images that grow as you write. *Then* **revise your lines into a consciously shaped poem. Consider both the original lines and the final poem. Open format**

One source of poetry lies within the individual poet: memories, experiences, and impressions (no matter how fleeting or evanescent). An intriguing way to release those possibilities is through free-association writing based on a recurrent phrase. The free-association allows the mind to explore its own directions; the recurrent phrase provides a sense of rudimentary form and structure, even at this early phase of creation.

A key to this exercise is to avoid 'writing' the poem too soon. Let the phrases emerge as they will. Then, when the raw materials have presented themselves, examine them for significant images, repeating ideas, nascent symbols that will allow themselves to be developed into a poem.

I. Original passage and revised poem:

Once I watched two sisters cry over their dying father.
Once I wanted to know what love really is.
Once I looked into my grandfather's scared eyes.
Once he took me fishing.
Once I sat in a hospital room and stared at his new bed.
Once I felt death sweep over me.
Once I dreaded growing old.
Once my mother taught me about family.
Once she made me proud to be her son.
Once I broke a promise to my parents.
Once they lost their trust in me.

Once I worked to make them proud of me.
Once I sacrificed my own desires to please them.
Once my mother held my hand as we boarded an airplane.
Once we left my grandfather for the last time.

ONCE

Once, standing next to my grandfather
on the streams of Colorado,
I stared into experienced eyes
and God watched over us.

Two sisters weeping,
my mother's tears wiped away
by the hand I held on an airplane
that flew us to a familiar land.

I witnessed death sweep over me
like an icy curtain.
Too many tears lost.
Strength needed in weak times.

Once, standing next to my grandfather
in a pale hospital room,
I stared into his fearful eyes
and God watched over him.

II. Original passage and revised poem:
ONCE

Once I slapped mom across the face.
Once I made myself throw up.
Once I ate Lucky Charms for three weeks.
Once I went to history class stoned.
Once I trusted...someone.
Once I kissed Duran Duran posters.
Once I moved away in ninth grade.
Once I took ballet lessons.

Once I slept with a bunny blanket over my head all night.
Once I cried when mom's boyfriend called me a slut.
Once I flashed my boobs at little boys in the swimming pool.
Once dad made me strip in front of the neighbors.
Once he called me a pansy ass.
Once I locked my sister in the closet for more than an hour.
Once I saw mom in bed with some strange guy.
Once I knew I'd never be like her.

I DO NOT THROW LIKE A GIRL, DAD

Stripped down
   to a mud matted tee
      and Mariners cap,

Freckled face
   hidden behind strands
      of dirt coated hair,

Waiting alone,
   tall and lanky,
      at the garage door,

Cotton candy toenails
   escaping tube socks
      onto bone cold pavement,

Ball clenched,
   Shoulders thrust back,
      in piercing-numb humility,

Mud play
   hosed away,
      leaving pink petals clinging to growing lumps.

III. Original passage and revised poem:

Once I stole candy from a discount store
Once I broke a promise and a leg
Once I ate Frosted Mini-Wheats
Once I sat up all night for Santa
Once I curled up with abdominal pains
Once I chased zebra
Once I cycled down Haleakala Crater
Once I swam with toe-fish
Once I burned twigs with a magnifying glass
Once I sought shelter in a corner
Once I read a book until I finished it
Once I tried to catch the wind in my jacket
Once I lied to a nun
Once I hid from my dad because he was drunk
Once I rolled bermuda grass into paper and tried to smoke
Once I thought I had appendicitis
Once I flew in an ultralight
Once I slept with my dog and got pneumonia
Once I pretended to care when I didn't
Once I pretended I didn't care when I did
Once I thought I was invincible
Once a bully kicked me in the chest
Once (Mom said) I almost burned down my house
Once I dug an underground fort in my backyard

ONCE

Once I caught wind in my jacket
gobbled the Frosted Mini-Wheat sky
and buzzed wild zebras and
Stewart who had kicked me in the chest
Once I took shelter in a corner
dad slurring screams of broken legs
and love and stolen candy and Brownie
and false appendicitis and damn liberals
Once I built a bunker in my sandbox

where I burned leaves and twigs
and the Bible through Job
until all I knew was smoke

IV. Original passage and revised poem
WHEN I SLEEP

When I sleep I always dream
When I sleep things are brighter
When I sleep I am comfortable
When I sleep there are no interrupting sounds
When I sleep I do not see myself
When I sleep the things that bother me disappear
When I sleep I dream in color
When I sleep it sometimes seems more real than life
 When I sleep problems disappear
When I sleep I enter a world that persists after awakening
When I sleep I am more at ease
When I sleep I am sometimes awakened by phantom sounds and
    touches
When I sleep I frequently wake up
When I sleep I need cold air even if it is snowing outside
When I sleep my bed becomes my cocoon
When I sleep I need weight across my feet
When I sleep I sometimes feel like a child again
When I sleep I toss and turn often
When I sleep it is sometimes 3 or 4 o'clock in the morning

MORE REAL THAN REAL

In my bed-cocoon I curl safely,
child-secure again,
dreaming Technicolor, surround-sound dreams
that burrow into the warmest convolutions
of my brain and shove aside,
sometimes roughly,
daytime thoughts.

In the icy-chilled night air
seeping over layered snow and through
cracked window sills,
a world more real than real
presents, revolves, reveals
itself, endures until
phantom voices, phantom fingertips
arouse me to a faded
listless place.

The following exercise in repetition has resulted in more than seventy shorter poems, many published online in several monthly issues of *Ygdrasil*:

REMEMBERY—

ONCE I tied a paring knife by the handle to a cellar beam and swung it back and forth until my father came downstairs, saw what I was doing, and strapped me with his belt;

ONCE I waited until my father was sitting on the toilet, then I went into the bathroom and kicked him in the shin to pay him back for strapping me with his belt;

ONCE I went fishing with an Idaho cousin and fouled my line in a half-drowned willow;

ONCE I collected three-inch hailstones in a cardboard box and was startled when they melted and flooded the garage;

ONCE I was frighted by my shadow on the wall as my parents painted our first house by the light of three shadeless lamps;

ONCE it rained so hard that the water flooded halfway u our front yard and our neighbors crossed the street in a rowboat;

ONCE we barely felt the Yellowstone earthquake and all of the neighbors were standing out on their front yards and when my father came home from a three-week field trip he wondered why everyone was outside to meet him;

ONCE my parents woke us up at 2AM and took us out onto the front step so that—once in our lives—we could see the Northern Lights ripple through the winter night;

ONCE I played school with my brother and two sisters in the basement all summer long;

ONCE I was sick for weeks because I was afraid I wouldn't get the fifth-grade teacher that I hoped for;

ONCE I hit a neighbor's little girl when I rode by on my first 26-incher and was convinced that I had killed her and hid in my bedroom for fear that her parents would kill me in return, only to find out that she wasn't even scratched and that her tricycle was unmarked;

ONCE I lived in a neighborhood where the parents would visit on lawn chairs on each others' front yards during long summer evenings, and all the ran around playing Horse;

ONCE my father brought home our Christmas tree in October and set it in a snow drift on the north side of the house and when he put it up it lasted for weeks without losing any needles;

ONCE my father bought another Christmas tree from a church group and we were disappointed because it looked so small and thin when he cut the twine binding it and then the next morning it was so big that he could barely get it up the stairs from the cellar and it took up almost a third of the living room;

ONCE I heard on the television that the Russians had sent up a satellite;

ONCE I had fifth grade with Miss Grafel and spent hours admiring her tables of African violets beneath the window;

ONCE I was running a relay-race for PE during the winter and one of the girls in my class ran right into me and knocked me over and the only thing that saved me from a concussion was my fur-lined parka hood;

ONCE I looked through my fourth-grade classroom door and saw Mrs. Robinson whack a student's hand with a ruler;

ONCE my sixth-grade teacher made me write with my left hand rubbing across the paper and the side of my hand was stained with black fountain-pen ink for weeks;

Once I walked to Burlington School in February and the snowdrifts were higher than my head and all we could see for the entire two miles was five-foot white drifts and the white-carpeted roadway;

Once we built a playhouse out of a hundred tumbleweeds towered on a slatted refrigerator carton and played in it for a week until our parents' discovered what we were doing and one of them made sure we were all out of the way and dropped a match onto the tumbleweeds and the entire playhouse exploded and burned to ashes within minutes;

Once we found a wild grapevine growing in the field behind our houses and one of us said that they were called "Lady Fingers" and we laughed at the name all the time we ate the long, sweet grapes;

Once my father showed us how to use a firecracker, a metal Minute-Maid orange juice can, and a tin pie plate filled with water to make a home-made rocket that could fly up a hundred feet;

Once we tried to make an igloo but couldn't make the snow hold up so we dug into the three-foot deep snow and made a fort anyway;

Once the sewers broke during the winter and flooded the entire block and all of the kids skated and sledded on it until one of the parents discovered what we were playing on and we all had to go inside until some fathers could lay a three-inch layer of ice over the sewage;

Once I had a garden on the side of the house and planted nicotine and butterfly wings

Initially, the *Remembery* poems were developed directly from images, phrases, and lines in this exercise piece; most frequently, a single line from the exercise became the core of a fourteen-line poem. By the midpoint of composition, however, the original exercise had triggered a number of other memories, sufficient to complete a sonnet-sequence.

2. SOURCES OF POETRY—VISUAL TRIGGERS

Write a poem based on the Payson eagle (or another visually intriguing sculpture or piece of standing art. Length: at least 12 lines. Form: open

Visual images can translate readily into poetry, particularly static images that allow the poet to examine them in detail. The statue in Payson Library, Pepperdine University, offers several hooks for poets: the curious quality of the carving; the juxtaposition of energy and stasis between the subject and the medium; and the inherent interest in eagle as metaphor, image, and symbol. Unfortunately, the same characteristics can lead to flat, stereotypic, convention-ridden, overly familiar treatments of eagles and poetry. In the hands of a master, however, something as common as an eagle can be transformed into powerful poetry, as in Alfred, Lord Tennyson's "The Eagle" or Walt Whitman's "The Dalliance of Eagles."

WRITING AN EAGLE POEM

We ring the statue—pens and pads
Raised like offerings to some exotic
God first unfurling wings to nod

At his humble worshippers. Idiotic
Content for a verse, this bird,
This misshapen, wooden, chaotic

Blend of scales and grains—absurd
In pose and posture, arced wings
Upswept in a static storm; immured

In its white-arc stucco niche, a thing
Unnatural and still—and from its angles
We must imagine lines that soar and sing.

THE EAGLE

The majestic eagle flies above us all,
Through mountain cathedrals soaring tall.
It symbolizes our nation's power and pride.
In its protection we do all abide.

We are blessed by its strong presence.
We share the strength of its grand essence.
But we do not treasure this great bird.
We let it's grandeur grow more slurred.

I look at this carved eagle statue.
It's beady eyes seem to stare back at you.
This eagle is a solid wooden key
To freedom here in Payson Library.

OPERATION IN A COUNTRY CHURCH

It bit, the sliver, burned to tender quick,
Slicing fingernail from moon-rise flesh.
It bit, the sliver, racing molten pricks
Up my arm, pain paired in ragged flashes.
Then deadness. Traitored nerves refused to play
Scarlet semaphores. Brain-muted echoes
Died.
      "Quick, while it's still numb," I heard him say
Softly. His bony hand gripped my elbow.
He cut, my grandfather, to tender quick,
Pared nail back to virgin, six-year flesh.
He cut, my grandfather, with his worn pocket-
Knife, deft, daring—our breath a fevered hush.
    Sliver, eagle-taloned, invading me;
    Strong eagle-blade to probe and let me free.

3. Sources of Poetry—Myth and Literature

Write a poem in which you use as the central figure a mythological being or beast that in turn represents a contemporary process, invention, etc. The poem must incorporate mythology concretely enough to define which being/beast you use, yet also define the contemporary analogue. 15-20 lines; Open form.

AND

Write a poem that *begins* by quoting a line or two from a poem in Drury or *TBAP* or another favorite contemporary poem. Your poem may accept or refute the assumptions implicit in the quoted lines but make the quotation integral to your own work. (After the poem, give an author/title/page reference for the quotation.) 15-20 lines; Open form

Writing out of responses to cultural stimuli often leads to poems that are at once personal and social, private and universal. Poets of all ages have looked back to the mythic and symbolic stories of the past, updating them and modifying them to give ancient images new power. Much of the strongest poetry of the Renaissance, for example, relied heavily on Classical mythology for images, motifs, stories, and ideas.

Similarly, contemporary poets can draw from earlier mythic cycles, including Classical (Greek and Roman), Egyptian, Norse, Eastern, Aztec/Mayan, and others. Drury quotes Linda Gregg's "Eurydice" as an example; John Milton's "Lycidas" depends on a complex structure of Classical and Christian mythology to achieve its purposes.

Response poetry similarly invites the poet into conversations with the past. The poet may freely borrow images, motifs, ideas, even lines and phrases from earlier poets, then move beyond those works to investigate the viability of older ideas. At times, this kind of quotation indicates the respect the later poet feels for the earlier. Richard Crashaw, for example, titled one of his collections *Steps to the Temple,* in conscious homage to George Herbert's *The Temple,* in spite of the fact that Crashaw's style differs widely from Herbert's. Henry Vaughan, on the other hand, did not hesitate to borrow rhyme schemes, rhythms, titles, even verbatim lines from Herbert, yet nevertheless manages to make each poem uniquely his own.

Examples of extended response-quotation poems include Christopher Marlowe's "The Passionate Shepherd to His Love" and the responses by Sir Walter Raleigh in "The Nymph's Reply to the Shepherd" and John Donne in "The Bait."

HOMMAGE: E.E. CUMMINGS

> Do you believe in always, the wind
> said to the rain
> I am too busy with
> my flowers to believe, the rain answered
> —e. e. cummings, "you said Is"

"I am too busy with
my flowers to believe,"

the (dripping
                    lightly)
rain   whispered (lightly)
           to flowers
al(a
   blo
   ssom
   unfolds
   meticulous
   gorgeousness)ways

lasts no longer than (how soon
                    petals weep
                    and drop)the scent

the lilacscent centered in the
    eye   the rosescent nestled securely
in the fingertips

al(gorgeousness
   conceals
   retreats
   to
   seed)ways
weighs the heavyweight of

breath

NOT HEEDING DAEDALUS WORDS ICARUS AGES

Flapping wings grown at birth
of scrapling wax and feathers
our ascent too outstanding an ambition
like Icarus in flight, the aging.
Soaring up, and higher, to the sun

thinking there is where the answers
are kept only getting near enough to
look down on your balding head
in realization that the feathers are gone.
There is no way to wing the sun has

stolen your sweet wax of youth
then the decent of screaming and
flailing dentures and a broken hip
trying only to wing again, resisting.
The sweet fall into the sea of rest.

BLINDNESS

Wake up and live now
scent of cut green blades.
try to block out the

brown sky infection,
and the pulseless there.
Upward emotion.
Flesh capacity,
health of a satchel,
needing not a scale.
Take shallower breaths.

The liquid is clear,
shake off intrusion.
Withdraw from the salt,
no gel of killers
can withstand to be.

Conflict no factor,
vibrations put forth.
Technology is.....
Ability is.....
so fear if you must.

Quoted from Bob Marley,
"Wake Up and Live"

AFTERLIFE

"And the Sun the Sun the
  Sun my visible father
  making my body visible
  thru my eyes!"

And the burning the burning the
  burning feeling grieved mother
  saw my body corrupt
  thru her eyes!

And the Moon the Moon the
  Moon full my Father
  washing my body clean

>   thru His eyes!
>
> And the glory the glory the
>   glory felt my King
>   had cleansed my body visible
>   thru my eyes!

"The Change: Kyoto-Tokyo Express"
by Allen Ginsberg

ROC

Wide wings, football-field wide,
Knotted with jets like seedpods
Swelling with cancers. Grey hide
Glisters sunlight above clouds,
Above air almost, before
It swoops morning-bright wings wide,
Drooping beneath the ice-grey door
Of dawn, to drop a single
Torpedo egg to earth.
Then up again on updrafts
Self-generated. And birth
Of death hatches bursts behind.

THE GREAT PRE-GOD CHAOS

Concretosaurus maximus gouges
    mouthful after starving mouthful
    barely pausing to
spit out tangled fibrous steel (*Con-max*
    has little need for roughage) then
    crunches another
girderspan, severs sinews, splays bone. It
    lunges punches gouges again—
    swallows pigeon-style
(neck taut, head extended) while dribbled dust
    settled like quake-loosened dandruff.

    Ravenously it
rips the fallen carcass, tears grey flesh…and
    Concretosaurus maximus
        sates its appetite

CREATION'S CHOIR

"The voice will expand to fill a given space.
As if to say, This space is not immeasurable."
My voice when left alone grows,
echo upon echo upon echo
until stretched out
it whispers,
gone.
Strain.
Cupped ear
traces returning tide.
Voice brought on Angel's wings
My voice with His forever flows,
Our voice will expand to fill all given space.
Saying, In grace the measured and immeasurable reside together.

Quotation by Michael Palmer's
Recursus (to Porta)

4. Cinquain

Write a cinquain, a syllabic form as follows (x represents a syllable):
   Line 1: x x
   Line 2: x x x x
   Line 3: x x x x x x
   Line 4: x x x x x x x x
   Line 5: x x
The form requires neither rhyme nor meter; however the final two-syllable line should emphasize the point of the poem, providing a pivotal irony that undercuts or underscores the preceding four lines.

Syllabics have the advantage of clear and easy structure coupled with potentially complex effects. Syllabic poems range from the surface simplicity of the haiku in its many English forms to the extraordinary polish of Dylan Thomas's "Fern Hill" [*TBAP* 632] and much of Marianne Moore's work, including "The Fish" [*TBAP* 462], in which syllable count leads to such abrupt lines as "ac-."

Of the fixed syllabic forms, the most common is the **haiku**. Originally the word *haiku* referred to the opening stanza of a long poem; as the three-line stanza gained in popularity, it separated from the rest of the poem and became a recognized form on its own. Its Japanese meaning remains simply "beginning." Perhaps its popularity arose because it is short and its traditional form precise: three lines, composed respectively of five syllables, seven, and five, although contemporary haiku no longer requires that poets follow this form rigidly, with results that include Ginsberg's famous one-liner [Drury 125]. Unfortunately the popularity of the form has also led to a great many haiku of indifferent quality; while the common practice of using it as an introduction to poetry in grade school— ostensibly because it is simplified enough for children to grasp easily—has created an animus against it for many readers. One study of children's reactions to poetry revealed that the two most unpopular forms among children were free verse (because of its lack of strong, obvious rhythm) and haiku.

For this exercise, then, you are invited to work with an alternate form, neither as popular as the haiku nor as familiar. The cinquain invites controlled pacing in the poem. Beginning with an abruptly short line, the poem expands until the eight-syllable fourth line; it then snaps back, often explosively, to two syllables. The tensions in the expanding/contracting lines can perfectly complement the subject, resulting in powerful but short poems. The form was first devised by Adelaide Crapsie; for an example of her work, see "Niagara" (Drury 62).

A related form, the Lanterne, presents an even greater challenge than the cinquain, since the number of syllables per line is cut in half:

    x
   xx
  xxx
 xxxx
    x

Here, any sense of meter dissipates, and the 'snap' from line to four to line five loses emphasis because line four is shorter and gains some because line five is a single, explosive syllable.

SNAP-BACK! CINQUAINS

Five lines;
Smooth left margin;
Words well-controlled, well-spelled;
Fourth line long, taut, and ready to
Snap back!

All with
Strict syllable
Count — undeviating
2 – 4 – 6 – 8 – then snap to 2 …
Surprise!

OUT OF ME

Mowing
Hills of green grass
With my father watching,
I grew tired. He took over
And fell

CAPTURED

Ta tum
Ta tum ta tum
Ta tum ta tum ta tum
Ta tum ta tum ta tum ta tum
set free

TO PLUNGE INTO AN UNKNOWN WORLD

mist grays
my world. waves pound
dry shakes. remembrances
drown ocean-wastes in deep-drawn breath…
I write.

YHWH

Till end
we shall see small
girl walking sorrow street
not death but toward horizons
Ceaseless.

CINQUAIN

For you
Two small symbols—
Red Roses in a vase
every Sunday morning on your
Tombstone.

HELLOCAUST

Pasty
White faces pressed
Against ice cold glass. Whisked
Helplessly along iron veins
To death.

BONUS EXERCISE
Having been forewarned of some of the dangers inherent in **haiku**, now try your hand at several, focusing on compression, elusive/allusive imagery, and verbal subtlety. Feel free to use the traditional 5-7-5 format or any of the more contemporary forms, as long as the poem hinges on image, incorporates nature as an element, and is as compressed as possible.

Examples:

ICE-BEARDED BASALT

Ice-bearded basalt
Haunts silent Snake River Gorge—
Old Men taunt old Tales

HAIKU: PHALAENOPSIS

Phalaenopsis
Wings have fluttered for a month—
Kitchen-window Grace

HAIKU: I GRAVITATE

I gravitate to
Haiku for their brevity—
*Hemerocallis**

> [**Hemerocallis*: The Day-lily—blooms throughout the summer, but each blossom lasts only one day.]

HAIKU: CONGREGATIONS OF GEESE

Congregations of
Geese surround the frozen pond:
December's Chapel

5. FIBONACCI SEQUENCE

A syllabic form with lines structured as follows (x indicates one syllable):
   Line 1: x
   Line 2: x
   Line 3: x x
   Line 4: x x x
   Line 5 x x x x x
   Line 6: x x x x x x x x
   Line 7: x x x x x x x x x x x x x

The practice in writing to imposed syllabic structures afforded by haiku and cinquains can, of course, be extended to other syllable-count structures. One of the most intriguing is based on a mathematical progression that itself presents something of a mystery. The Fibonacci sequence, simply defined, is a series of numbers, each formed of sum of the two preceding numbers: 1, 1, 2, 3, 5, 8, 13, 21, 34, 55, 89, and so forth. The sequence has provided mathematicians with some intriguing data. In *The Fragile Species* (1992), Lewis Thomas spends several paragraphs meditating upon the peculiarities inherent in the Fibonacci sequence:

> ...the ratio of any number to the preceding one is the famous irrational number 1.618034, while its ratio to the next one up is 0.618034. This relationship defines the so-called golden section, on which architecture has relied for its traditional aesthetic, and which defines the growth of trees, the replication of rabbits, the spirals of seeds in sunflowers and the fronds of pine cones, and even, as I have recently read in a learned paper by an incomprehensible (to me) Hungarian musicologist, the composition of Bartók.

Generations of amateurs have puzzled over the Fibonacci sequence and its endless ramifications, even since Leonardo Fibonacci set it up in the thirteenth century. I have filled a notebook with my own "discoveries," all doubtless discovered by others a hundred or more years ago. Like this: 322 (or 321.9) multiplied by any number in the series will give (roughly) the twelfth number ahead in the series; the square root of 322 gives the sixth number ahead; the cube root gives three numbers ahead; the fourth root gives a number 3.3301 times the first number back, and so forth.

Add up all the digits in a Fibonacci number, and reduce this sum to a single digit, as follows: 10,946 (which happens to be the twenty-first number)=20=2. Now do the same with the twelfth number back from 10,946, which is 34, or the twelfth ahead, which is 3,524,578, and you will find that these digits sum to 7. Thus, the digits in every pair of Fibonacci numbers, twelve apart, have the sum of 9, whether 7+2, or 5+4, or 6+3, or 8+1. Moreover, these reduced digits, when lined up, display a regular, absolutely reproducible cycle, every twenty-four Fibonacci numbers, no matter how big the numbers become.

Someone knows for sure why these things are so, and proper mathematicians can no doubt prove the empirical facts by equations, but I don't care. For my purposes, the Fibonacci series keeps my mind quiet—not at peace, for that would be too much to ask for, but quiet at least. And, I might add, something distantly related, as my mind sees it, to the sound of music.

All sense of mystery aside, Thomas identifies the characteristics of a curious sequence—not the least being its affinity to music…and to poetry.

As a counting device, the Fibonacci sequence is particularly applicable to poetry, especially beginning poetry. It provides a natural structure that avoids the over-familiarity of haiku (and the difficulties inherent in questions of linguistic and cultural translation in relation to form), and the sometimes too-abrupt curtness of the cinquain. And since most of the lines contain odd-numbers of syllables, the Fibonacci allows—if not *forces*—writers to break from the underlying iambic rhythms of English.

Even though it is an open-ended sequence, there is a natural limit to the lengths a poet can take it within a single poem. Beyond seven lines—when the syllable count reaches 13—the lines become cumbersome and bulky. It is, indeed, difficult (although not impossible) to imagine poetic lines of 34, 55, or 81 syllables. Of course, additional length is available by either using the 5-7 line Fibonacci as a stanza form, or by reversing the sequence, producing a two-part poem with a syllable count such as 1-1-2-3-5-8-13—13-8-5-3-2-1-1. As a straightforward means of structuring a poem, however, the sequence provides a ready-made lesson in the relation between line length and a sense of bulk or weight, as in this poem:

GENEALOGY

Her
Hands
Fold air—
Arthritic
Hands of ninety-four
And more....Snow-bit winter air claws
Through her hands to snatch at breast and bone and drag her
    home.

CRESCENDO AND DECRESCENDO

Dark
adds
to black;
compounds add;
chemicals react
and chain frail life-engendering
daisy links suffusing elements that will be worlds.

Histories compress and life becomes a memory
Etched in stones that burn in solar
Flares and boil away;
Stars remain
Until
The
End

DUSK

Dusk
flirts
with bright
contours—flame-
pink, red, orange drain
mote-energies through dying day....

Grey-
blue
and calm,
wings enfold
brightness—somber dusk
draws silent sleep through muted night....

DAWN/BURSTS

Dawn
Bursts
Darkness,
Rises with
Triumphal ardor,
Strains through cool blues of fruitful Day

                                                  And
                                                 Soars
                                            Beyond
                                    Heaven's Crown,
                                  Embraces with light
                      Bright regions of sweet Summer Stars.

FÊTE

Dew forms silver apples on marbled quartz tiles, fragile
crystal goblets sit awaiting
masked humanity--
parasols

aside
for
now.

I C U

Wires
Tubes
Machine
Pump Pumping
Lips twitch tight whispers
Shadow-words sleep in tunnelled eyes
Stiff, bone grip cries as machine stutters beep-shush-beep-shush...

OAK FLATS MORNING

Soft
Mist
Dissolves
In the glow
Of dawn, revealing
Weathered oak silhouettes, specters
Looming like memories in the sticky morning fog.

METER

> "It is possible to distinguish various degrees of relative syllabic stress in English speech, but the most common and generally useful fashion of analyzing and classifying the standard English meters is to distinguish only two categories of stress in syllables—weak stress and strong stress—and to group the syllables into metric feet according to the patterning of these two stresses. A **foot** is the combination of a strong stress and the associated weak stress or stresses which make up the recurrent metric unit of a line. The relatively stronger-stressed syllable is called, for short, 'stressed'; the relatively weaker-stressed syllables are called 'light,' 'slack,' or simply 'unstressed.'" —M. H. Abrams, *A Glossary of Literary Terms*.

A key term in Abrams' definition is *relatively*. In general, in any pair of adjacent syllables in English, one will receive more *relative* stress. The line, "Rain yesterday, and I, afraid," might be described as iambic tetrameter—four feet using an unstressed-stressed pattern.

In actual practice, "Rain" will probably receive a fair level of stress, since it is an initial noun; yet *relative* to the next syllable, it receives less stress, creating an iambic foot: "Rain yes-." Similarly, in *relative* terms, "-ter-" receives slightly less stress than "-day"; "and" substantially less than "I"; and "a-" less than "-fraid." Thus, instead of a metronomic iambic reading—"Rain yesterday, and I, afraid," which would in fact strain normal English pronunciation—the line responds more fluidly and naturally, while still retaining an underlying iambic rhythm, if read using several levels of *relative* stress: "Rain **yes-**/-ter<u>day</u>,/ and **I**,/ a<u>fraid</u>."

The four most common metrical feet in English are:

1. IAMB—an unstressed followed by a stressed syllable:
    'Tis hard to say, if greater Want of Skill
    Appear in Writing or in *Judging* ill....
                                            —Alexander Pope,

from *An Essay on Criticism*

2. ANAPEST—two unstressed syllables followed by one stressed syllable:
>The Assyrian came down like a wolf on the fold,
>And his cohorts were gleaming in purple and gold....
>>—George Gordon, Lord Byron,
>>"The Destruction of Sennacherib"

3. TROCHEE—one stressed syllable followed by one unstressed syllable:
>>Rinsed like something sacrificial
>>Ere 'tis fit to touch our chaps....
>>>—Robert Browning,
>>>"Soliloquy of the Spanish Cloister"

4. DACTYL—one stressed syllable followed by two unstressed syllables:
>>Half a league, half a league,
>>Half a league onward....
>>>—Alfred, Lord Tennyson,
>>>"The Charge of the Light Brigade"

Following these four are several others, used primarily as substitutions rather than for entire lines. Each adds specific effects to a poetic line.

5. SPONDEE—two equally stressed syllables constituting a single foot; often used as a substitution to retard the movement of a line:
>>Rocks, Caves, Lakes, Fens, Bogs, Dens, and shades of death
>>>—John Milton,
>>>*Paradise Lost,* Book II.592

6. PHYRRIC—two equally unstressed syllables; often used as a substitution to quicken the line:
>>After the style of Virgil and of Homer,

So that my name of Epic's no misnomer....
—George Gordon, Lord Byron,
Don Juan, Canto I, Stanza CC

7. AMPHIBRACH—one unstressed syllable, one stressed syllable, and one unstressed syllable; generally substituted in an iambic or trochaic line:
Di-vi-sive; Col-la-tion

8. AMPHIMACER—one stressed syllable, one unstressed syllable, and one stressed syllable; generally substituted an iambic or trochaic line:
Comp-li-ment (verb; note that the noun is dactyllic: Comp-li-ment)

Metrical feet, it will be noted, are determined regardless of word breaks or punctuation. A single word may cross the boundaries of three or more separate feet, assuming a multisyllabic word. Similarly, a foot might bridge the space created by a comma, semi-colon, or other mark of punctuation. The crucial factor is the *relative* stress between two adjacent syllables.

Metrical feet are traditionally arranged by number to create lines:
One foot = MONOMETER
Two feet = DIMETER
Three feet = TRIMETER
Four feet = TETRAMETER
Five feet = PENTAMETER
Six feet = HEXAMETER
Seven feet = HEPTAMETER
Eight feet = OCTAMETER

To define meter, we identify the predominant foot and the number of feet per line, *e.g.*, 'iambic pentameter,' 'anapestic trimeter.' A poem in iambic pentameter may in fact have only slightly more than half of its lines in strict iambs, as long as the meter continues to provide an undercurrent of iambic rhythm for the poem. Similarly, poems may be constructed of lines in varying feet, providing interesting shifts in rhythm, pacing, and patterning.

OTHER IMPORTANT TERMS:

Unrhymed IAMBIC PENTAMETER—**Blank Verse**
IAMBIC HEXAMETER—**Alexandrine**
IAMBIC HEPTAMETER—**Poulter's Measure, also called Fourteeners.**
   Such lines generally break into four feet followed by three feet.
      Example: "The Wife of Usher's Well" [Drury 109]

DISCUSSIONS OF METER IN METER:

S. T. Coleridge, METRICAL FEET—*LESSONS FOR A BOY*

Trochee trips from long to short;
From long to long in solemn sort
Slow spondee stalks; strong foot! yet ill able
Ever to come up with Dactyl trisyllable.
Iambics march from short to long—
With a leap and a bound the swift Anapests throng;
One syllable long, with one short at each side,
Amphibrachys hastes with a stately stride—
First and last being long, middle short, Amphimacer
Strikes his thundering hoofs like a proud high-bred racer.
If Derwent* be innocent, steady, and wise,
And delight in the things of earth, water, and skies;
Tender warmth at his heart, with these meters to show it,
With sound sense in his brain, may make Derwent a poet—
May crown him with fame, and must win him the love
Of his father on earth and his Father above.

My dear, dear child!
Could you stand upon Skiddaw, you would not from its whole
   ridge
See a man who so loves you as your fond S.T. COLERIDGE.

ON STRESS

In olden days, the sonnet's lines were built
With care to make the reader rise and fall
While ambling through the splendid, gaudy gilt
Of words in rhythms that must never stall;

In strictest forms, each line was fit with care
Into a predetermined march of stress;
Down, up, down, up—they strode with polished flair,
Creating their own forward-moving press.

But now—ah now!—poets may feel more free,
May shift their stresses—lightly—if they please,
Until sound and meaning cogently agree,
And meter echoes form with pleasant ease.

Still, under all, the heart-beat throbs persist,
Incessant, too demanding to resist.

While understanding the mechanics of meter is invaluable to a poet, especially valuable is the ability to keep meter from overwhelming the poem. Alexander Pope gave some solid advise on how to write (and some excellent examples at the same time) in his lengthy discussion of "numbers" (meter) in *An Essay on Criticism* (ll. 285-380).

Merely understanding meter is usually not sufficient to guarantee that a particular meter will work in a particular poem. One of the most interesting examples of an unwieldy tension between meter and content occurs in one of the earliest English tragedies. According to one scholar, "Thomas Preston's *Cambises, King of Persia*, although almost totally devoid of any real literary merit, is one of the most interesting plays of mid-sixteenth century England" (Nethercot and others, *Elizabethan Plays*). Unfortunately, part of that interest lies in the uncomfortable juxtaposition of a rapid, swinging rhythm and solemn, tragic, at times melodramatic content:

Thomas Preston, from CAMBISES, KING OF PERSIA

[Mother]: Alas, alas I do hear tell the king hath killed my son!
If it be so, woe worth the deed that ever it was done!....
O blissful babe! O joy of womb! Heart's comfort and delight!
For counsel given unto the king is this thy just requite?
O heavy day and doleful time, these mourning tunes to make!
With blubbered eyes, into mine arms from earth I will thee take...
                     [continues thus for eighteen more lines]

For poetry, concerns of sound and sense may include the presentation of poetry as well as its composition, an issue that became a standard element in rhetorical and oratorical theory in the nineteenth and early twentieth centuries. While contemporary poets may be less focused on matters of elocution and verbal flourish, awareness of how poems may *sound* still matters.

S. S. Hamill's *The Science of Elocution* (1884) and Albert N. Raub's *The New Normal Fifth Reader* (1878, 1894) both contain the following advice for performing poetry and prose:

Lloyd, EXPRESSION IN READING

'Tis not enough the voice be sound and clear—
'Tis modulation that must charm the ear.
When desperate heroines grieve with tedious moan,
And whine their sorrows in a see-saw tone,
The same soft sounds of unimpassioned woes
Can only make the yawning hearer doze.
That voice all modes of passion can express
Which marks the proper word with proper stress;
But none emphatic can the reader call
Who lays an equal emphasis on *all*.

Some o'er the tongue the labored measures roll
Slow and deliberate as the parting toll;

Point every stop, mark every pause so strong,
Their words like stage-processions stalk along.
All affectation but creates disgust,
And even in speaking we may seem *too* just.
In vain for them the pleasing measure flows,
Whose recitation runs it all to prose;
Repeating what the poet sets not down,
The verb disjoining from its friendly noun,
While intonation, pause, and break combine
To make a discord in each tuneful line.

Some placid natures fill the allotted scene
With lifeless drone, insipid and serene;
While others thunder every couplet o'er
And almost crack your ears with rant and roar.
More nature oft and finer strokes are shown
In the low whisper than tempestuous tone,
And Hamlet's hollow voice and fixed amaze
More powerful terror to the mind conveys
Than he who, swollen with big impetuous rage,
Bullies the bulky phantom off the stage.

He who in earnest studies o'er his part
Will find true nature cling about his heart.
The modes of grief are not included all
In the white handkerchief and mournful drawl;
A single look more marks the internal woe
Than all the windings of the lengthened *O!*
Up to the face the quick sensation flies,
And darts its meaning from the scornful eyes;
Love, transport, madness, anger, scorn, despair,
And all the passions, of the soul, is there.

While the poet is obviously aware of Pope's discussion of "sound and sense," "Expression in Reading" lacks both Pope's ability to incorporate content with form and Pope's facility with the heroic couplet; in spite of its good advice for oral performance of poems,

Lloyd's work remains didactic rather than poetic, simple rather than sophisticated. Throughout, the requirements of his subject matter take precedence over poetry, resulting in strained syntax and self-conscious lines.

Some final thoughts on metered verse:

IN DEFENSE OF FORM: AN EPISTLE IN THE MANNER OF ALEXANDER POPE

For Amera and Ecrivain 01

Some think of form as but a poet's crutch,
Good for structure, but for else, not much.
They hold that all good modern verse is 'free,'
Let each line choose how it will look and be.
They say that forms will stifle all invention,
And all who use them should be in detention.
Naysayers such as these might never know
The elegance well-crafted forms can show,
And look on form-verse as a poet's foe.
    Now, free-form has its place in modern verse;
Its lines can be quite supple, taut, and terse.
In Eliot's master's-hands, or Williams's,
Free-verse can work as well as form-verse does.
But all too often lesser hands confuse
Such vivid brilliance with more mundane hues;
Without a clear poetics as a guide,
Free-verse becomes an uncontrolled, wild ride.
Lines stutter with no sense of calm repose,
And poems seem but random, chopped-up prose.
Some poems spread themselves across the page,
As if a poet's word-hoard, burst in rage;
While others slither down the left-hand side,
As if in some precarious word-slide.
And others lie page-center for no good cause,
Except to shape a needless, ragged vase

Or pull attention from its inner flaws.
    But from the proper pen, a form can ring,
And, like a well-tuned bell, both chime and sing.
    The Sonnet moves with elegant, poised grace,
A 'little song' embraced by pristine space;
For nearly a thousand years its subtle power
Has guided countless poets through its bower;
And though our modern, jaded tastes might sneer
At arbitrary-seeming rules, austere
And exquisite, great sonnets still appear.
    The Villanelle, through rustic in its name,
When well-conceived, can bring its author fame;
It's repetons incant their stately might,
And rise, when strong, to Dylan's "gentle night."
    The Cinquain, brief but pithy, builds its lines
In strictly mathematical designs,
Its syllables expand in even track
Until the final short line snaps us back.
    Chaucer's ancient lines, in "Royal Rhyme,"
Recall to us a distant, older, time;
Kings chose to write in this stanzaic form,
But even moderns use it as their norm.
    Sweet Haiku, nature joined to image, dare
Poets to be emblematic, spare;
In seventeen crisp increments of sound,
They elevate what's common to profound.
    And on it goes, in limitless array:
From witty Clerihew to Triolet;
Acrostics, with their dual messages,
The Etheree, with childhood vestiges.
Pantoum and Quatrain, Rondel, Rondelet,
Anacreontics, Limericks…and yet….
When wit and talent, word and form are married
The world of verse stays infinitely varied.

EXERCISES

6. "SLOTH" IMITATION

> Write a poem modeled on Theodore Roethke's "The Sloth." Use the same stanza, rhyme scheme, and comic tone. Select an *animal* as your subject. Twelve lines; iambic tetrameter; rhyme scheme AAA BBB CCC DDD

Here is an opportunity to use rhyme and meter overtly, obviously, and comically—in fact, the heavier the rhyme and meter, the better. Because of the emphasis on technique, this exercise invites lightness of tone, particularly when the chosen animal itself seems semi-comic. On the other hand, because so much of the effect depends on careful manipulation of rhyme and rhythm, any flaws in either may seriously weaken the poem, as threatens in the following example:

WOLF

Stalwart and steadfast is my mate
Has a spectral white glow to sate
The lecherous heart, who knows fate.

Loves lagniappe sundered chicken flesh.
He mauls and lauds his work as lech.
Runs wild shimmering tempts to catch.

He treks as trencherman on the plains
Infernal beast, zephyr in manes.
He knows no limit to his lanes.

Devoid, devout, deposer, demiser
Seeks to delude for he's kisser
Running in packs, leads as demiser.

Robert Herrick's "Upon Julia's Clothes" uses the same rhyme and meter in a shorter poem that explores a vastly different range of emotions:

> Whenas in silks my *Julia* goes,
> Then, then (me thinks) how sweetly flows
> That liquefaction of her clothes.
>
> Next, when I cast my eyes and see
> That brave Vibration each way free;
> O how that glittering taketh me!

In spite of the differences between Herrick's verse and Roethke's, note the similar crucial use of key multi-syllabic words: *ex-as-per-at-ing* in Roethke, *li-qui-fac-tion, vi-bra-tion,* and *glit-ter-ing* in Herrick.

Other poems based on animals (though using different forms) include Emily Dickinson's "I Heard a Fly Buzz—When I Died" and "A Narrow Fellow in the Grass"; E. J. Pratt, "The Prize Cat" [*TBAP* 427]

Which of the following manage to control and exploit rhythm and rhyme?

THE ROACH

> Historically, he's quite antique,
> With forebears who would wryly peek
> At dinosaurs, then—scuttling—sneak
>
> Into dark cracks. But to this date
> He still survives in unchanged state
> (Though smaller, thank God!) to irritate
>
> New-comer men, who daily try
> To make new ways to make him die,
> And, giving up, sit back and cry

While he and his cohorts slyly approach
Dark kitchen drawers, and like a coach,
Race in tandem, roach by roach.

ORANGUTAN

Sophisticated, this urbanite
has never heard of working, quite,
too busy dozing day and night.

Long hairy arms like hempen rope,
he ponders fate and swings and mopes;
ancestral kin to kids on dope—

A puff of lazy life's decay,
he hasn't moved since yesterday;
tomorrow, too, he'd slip away.

But no, this repast hangs in vain,
his selfish trait just can't restrain
those female guiles and hunger pains.

TRIASSIC

A splashing sound a mile away,
a blond and sunburned child at play,
my sense of smell is good today!

I slide below the hanging feet,
the sticks of skin and bones and meat,
to taste the salty flesh so sweet.

I use the day for bump and run,
to put a cloud on someone's fun,
then I choose who'll be the one.

Food that flees is good for me,
I close my jaws and then I see,

he who surfs has ceased to be.

CHESTER THE CENTAUR

When speaking of a Centaur's rear,
You must never quite appear
Too cognizant of what shows here;

The human foreparts may profess
Inordinate pride--more or less--
In equine curves you there address.

He'll swish a regal, coiffured tail,
Nor ever once pretend to fail
To notice compliments--but pale

And rage should ever it so pass
That you, in ignorance, slip—alas!—
And foolishly speak of a *horse's* ass!

THE HUMMINGBIRD

Your whirring wings weary the eye,
Drinking the nectar as you fly
As if the flowers will soon run dry.

(Smarter flowers soon would see
Your thirsting promiscuity
And ask you kindly for a fee).

A slave to the organ in your chest,
You'll never know the meaning of rest—
You cannot stop and take a breath!

Without a fix your wings won't beat—
Deceived by color you pause to eat
But sugar is sweet and sweet is sweet.

BONUS EXERCISE

Try your hand at answering Herrick's encomium on his mistress (who, although he wrote many poems about her, was entirely imaginary. Work within his rhythms, rhyme, and form, trying to establish an overriding and consistent tone.

Example:

UPON JULIA UNCLOTHED

Though liquefaction may suffice,
In silks, to beckon and entice
And humble nature with device;

Yet silkless beauty can compare
And tender glories just as rare
In shoulders smooth and bosoms bare.

7. REVISION

Select one poem written thus far for this handbook and revise it completely to make it the most effective poem you can; since this is a revision rather than a correction, you must alter the poem in substantive ways: length, scope of content, poetic form or structure (e.g., change a free verse original into a rhymed metrical poem), etc.

One of the most extraordinary examples of revision occurs in the poems by Marianne Moore titled "Poetry." Only half a dozen lines long in its original version, the poem expanded over Moore's career, resulting eventually in thirty syllabic lines [*TBAP* 461]. In her final version, however, published at the end of her life, she revised the poem radically, almost reproducing her original [*TBAP* 462]. What has been added in the revision? What, if anything, has been lost?

MORE REAL THAN REAL

In my bed-cocoon I curl safely,
child-secure again,
dreaming Technicolor, surround-sound dreams
that burrow into the warmest convolutions
of my brain and shove aside,
sometimes roughly,
daytime thoughts.

In the icy-chilled night air
seeping over layered snow and through
cracked window sills,
a world more real than real
presents, revolves, reveals
itself, endures until
phantom voices, phantom fingertips
arouse me to a faded
listless place.

MORE REAL THAN REAL [revision]

In my bed-cocoon I safely curl,
secure in Technicolor swirls,
surround-sound dreams that push aside
dull, boring thoughts where suns abide.

Through ice-chilled air from window sills,
A world more real than real fills
My dreaming mind, till a phantom face
Returns me to my listless place.

SURVIVAL CAMP I

Awakening at four AM;
Mirrored Orions (lake to sky) stalked
Restless stars

I kept breathless watch,
Against my stone backrest,
Its lichen covering

Palms pressed sharply,
Flesh enfolded glittering
Mica flakes

Light breeze rippled
Haunting
Across the lake

SURVIVAL CAMP II

awake at four o'clock;
onyx-mirrored Orions (lake to sky) still stalked
unweary stars

I kept breathless watch,
barely felt my roughened granite backrest,
its silvered lichen filaments

naked palms pressed sharply,
my wanting flesh enfolded glinting mica
granules

a light breeze rippled
(ripples) hauntingly
from the east

this is the rock where sleep would not come,
where campfire-hum and mosquito-flicker
alike

silently declined to moistly nurturing

darkness,
lit only by the passing motions of crisp stars
stark phoenix-flames of my imagination

BONUS EXERCISE

Select any poem in this handbook thus far and revise it (knowing that your perceptions and expectations will not be exactly those of the author). Concentrate on vividness of language and image, on compression, on music and patterning. At the same time, try to remove any unnecessary (to you) words or phrases that might detract from the poems overall effect.

SURVIVAL CAMP III

onyx-mirrored Orions (lake to sky)
stalk unweary stars

I kept breathless watch,
naked palms pressed sharply,
against glinting mica

this is the rock where sleep
would not come,
mosquito-flicker

silently declined to darkness,
lit only by crisp stars
stark phoenix-flames

THE EAGLE I

The majestic eagle flies above us all,
Through mountain cathedrals soaring tall.
It symbolizes our nation's power and pride.
In its protection we do all abide.

We are blessed by its strong presence.
We share the strength of its grand essence.
But we do not treasure this great bird.
We let it's grandeur grow more slurred.

I look at this carved eagle statue.
It's beady eyes seem to stare back at you.
This eagle is a solid wooden key
To freedom here in Payson Library.

EAGLES II

Eagles wheel above
Cathedral-stones in wild flight—
We share deep essence

8. METRICAL IMITATIONS

(a). Write a poem based on Robert Frost's "A Dust of Snow." Follow the line lengths, syllable count, metrics, rhyme-scheme, and stanza form precisely, using your own subject and words. Try to achieve the same variation in mood that Frosts attains. 8 lines, iambic dimeter, ABAB CDCD

AND

(b). Write a double dactyl: two quatrains with the two last lines of each stanza rhyming. Except for the truncated rhyming lines, all lines are dactylic dimeter. The first line is a double dactyl nonsense word ("Higgledy-Piggledy" for example.) The second line must be a double dactyl name. The antepenultimate line consists of a one-word double dactyl line. The double dactyl was devised and refined by John Hollander and Anthony Hecht in *Jiggery-Pokery*.

Short, strongly metrical rhyming poetry may be powerful, as in Frost's "A Dust of Snow" or Robert Graves' *cynghanedd* [Drury 306]. Extended, short rhythmic rhyming lines may echo John Skelton's Skeltonics [Drury 257-258]. Such forms can also, however, become easily parodic and/or comic, simply because of the *insistent* rhythm and rhyme. One such form, called the "Terse-Verse" (for obvious reasons), attempts to reduce longer, more solemn (and better known) poems to their illogical essence in eight lines of iambic dimeter:

E. A. POE'S "THE RAVEN": A Terse Verse

Black Bird
abjured
was heard
by Nerd;

Black Bird

> preferred
> long Word
> absurd.

In the Frost paraphrase, try to communicate significance and complexity through an apparently simple structure; in the double dactyl, just have fun.

FROST'S CROW, REAPPEARING

A wayward Crow
By a frozen lea
Seems a sable foe
With a sinister plea,

And gives a start,
That drives me to brood
Over injuries' smart
And choices long rued.

NECTARINE

The nectarine,
pale purple-pink
with springtime sheen,
seems to wink

its blossom-eyes;
while carefree larks
assert the lie
of winter's darks.

THE WAY A STONE

The way a stone
Returned to me
A glance of foam
From a stormy sea

Revealed the weave
Of Nature's grace
On a grief-filled Eve
To a tear-stained face.

A SPRINGTIME RAIN

A springtime rain
Startles the sky—
Dissuades bright clouds
From scudding by—

Presses them
To pause a while—
And bead slight gems
In single file

DRIVING ALONE IN THE DESERT, EAGER FOR THE DAWN

On cut-out hills
A mottled pink
Hides with frills
The sun's shy wink;

Then grows into
A deeper flush
That paints pale dew
With a glittering brush.

DAISIES' GOLD

The daisies' gold
Has given way
To grey-washed clouds
At close of day—

By highways damp
With scattered rain,

Frail springtime's lamps
Grow dim again….

ATROPHY

When I, the dark
had ceased to feel
the madness, stark
came for its meal.

So dimmed, the mind
went forth unheard,
a gnawing grind,
the dark, a word.

THE MORNING FROST

The bite of rain
On slender lips
The sinking pain
In her fingertips

Has silenced the heath
Alert to screams
And lifts relief
In dispersing steam

(B). DOUBLE DACTYL

SOME DOUBLE-DACTYL WORDS:

uncomplimentary
duplicability
supercollectible
heterosexual
Mediterranean
irreproducible
memorabilia
circumlocutional
unsuitability
unenterprisingly
anticlimactical
psychoanalysis
extemporaneous
extraterrestrial

veterinarian
phantasmagorical
characteristically
scientifictional
microbiology
Mesopotamian
antepenultimate
counterintelligence
universality
nymphomaniacal
heliocentrical
uncharismatically
sesquicentennial

SOME DOUBLE-DACTYL NAMES:

Juliet Capulet
Ralph Waldo Emerson

Romeo Montague
Vladimir Nabokov

EXAMPLES:

EDUCATING MORALITY

Higgledy-piggledy
Some universities
Counsel that Christians
Don't smoke and don't drink.

Laudable attitudes—
If students going there
Characteristically
Learn how to think.

SCHOOL OF HARD KNOCKS

Rickety-rackety
Grandmother Washington
Taught all her children to
Knit and crochet,

Thumping and bumping
With thimble-capped fingers she
Uncompromisingly
Made them obey.

MILITARY DISCIPLINE

Bumpity-Jumpity
General Harrington
Woke up at dawn in a
Juvenile mood

Smugly he ordered his
Disciplined army to
Quasi-robotically
March in the nude

KING HENRY THE EIGHTH

Luckity-Duckity
Catherine of Aragon
lost her religion but
rescued her life.

Her brotherly husband
characteristically
hacked off the head of his
next lovely wife.

JACKAROO'S LAST RIDE

Gallupy-Sallupy
Kimberly Jackaroo
Rode on a stallion to
town to say hi.

Instead she held up the
market with pistols and
unenterprisingly
stole a pot pie.

BONUS EXERCISE:

Select another poet with a distinctive style and voice and, as closely as possible, imitate the metrical and verbal patterns in his or her poems.

Example: Emily Dickinson

AGATE SLICE

Over eons, crystals weep
Their microscopic tears—
In crevice cut and cavern deep
They count their dolesome years

By evanescent layers laid—
An infinite array
Of milk and cream and snow-cascade—
Invisible display

Until an enterprising hand
Plays lapidary sleuth—
The slice unveils a crimson band
Of elemental truth—

IN THE GARDEN, SWEET-HEARTS GROW—

In the garden—Sweet-Hearts grow—
A single branching stem—
Not waiting for a spring-time thaw—
Or Bumblebee's soft Hum—

But thrusts—a snow-bound visitor—
Into ice-frigid air—
An isolate Inquisitor—
A purple-tinted Spear—

It stands above the hoarfrost line—
It sways—on wayward Wind—
Extends its hearts in trust—and then
Offers them to lend—

None can own them—none possess—
But bear them—as a Gift—
For they are brittle—as sharp Glass—
And easy to be cleft—

ELEMENTAL SONG

White tray of Flesh—white tray of Blood—
Deathly grasped-by-hand—
Water clear and parted Bread—
Thrown-together—dressed—

Touch our Lips to christian-care—
Touch our Tongues to troth—
Taste—with life-tool never born—
Still separacies of Love—

White trays pass on—clear water dims—
Bread sleeps—only bread—
Wake anew—in Child-hood—
This come-together—fit—

BONUS EXERCISE

Select an artist from a genre other than writing—painting, dance, music, etc.—and write a poem that expresses that artist's style in words.

Example: Jackson Pollack

HOMMAGE: JACKSON POLLACK

I saw him once—on film—
painting on glass   camera
poised beneath to capture
spatterswirlcoilflash
colorshapetexture

as paint flew—faster than vision—
onto glass   lines
perfectly obedient to his wish
placedspaced
sharpenedshaped

anyone could do that—someone smirked—
but   no   his
brushed moved too carefully   to
handeyearmbody
imagevisionmagic

what emerged—not madness—
but method art
chaos in my world
controlledmodifiedarticulated
transformed to form

Example: Gian Lorenzo Bernini

THE ECSTASY OF S. TERESA DI AVILA

Bernini captured it: ecstatic, wreathing
Exultation … exhalation … pain
Severing into heart and core … breathing
Moans unutterable, as if hot veins
Were suddenly transmuted into gold,
Molten ore more richly vibrant than
The golden spear the vision thrust with bold
Diligence thrice into her flesh…again…
And yet again. Sweet agony…fire-
Borne bliss…. Solid marble writhes and gasps,
Grasps in earthly elements a higher
Adoration than bitter breath can rasp:
    Not in its surcease could she know true peace.
    Nor would she wish such sovereign pain to cease.

9. GWENDOLYN BROOKS IMITATION

Write a poem imitating Gwendolyn Brook's "We Real Cool." Select a group of people you know and have observed, and create an image that communicates their essence.

Note how effectively Brooks' transposition of words shifts the rhythms and stresses in her poem. Had she chosen to begin each line with the repeated "We," each would have constituted a single amphimacer (excepting the last), with rather blunt aa bb cc dd rhyme. By shifting "we" to the ends of lines 2-7, she instead creates a poem in which nearly every syllable receives stress, the strong masculine rhymes are pocketed in the middle of each line, and the repeated "we" gains incremental stress with each appearance.

Try playing with the form to see if other variations add or detract from the power of the form. Decide whether the lines sound normal or forced, meaningful or tangential.

WE NO FOOLS

The last of the Mammoth hunters, 10,000 B.C.

We no fools. We
kill bulls. We

kill cows. We
know Nows. We

want kills. We
watch hills. We

watch lea. We
no see. We

watch moon. We
starve soon.

THEY LIKE SNOW

The six across the street, throwing behind their forts.

They like snow. They
can throw. They

make balls. They
take falls. They

wet clothes. They
'slay' foes. They

no mice. They
lob ice. They.

play bold. They
sleep cold.

ONE WEARS PINK

Five on the way to a late-night party.

One wears pink. She
won't think. One

wears blue. She's
still new. One

wears grey. She's
from away. One

wears plaid. She's
so bad. One

wears gold. She's
too old.

Compression I: Saying Much with Little

Some practical suggestions for tightening bulky lines—Eliminating Unnecessary Prepositions

Characteristically, poems tend toward compression. One hallmark of great poetry is that it communicates much more than the total of its words. Diction, image, metaphor, symbol—all combine to give poetry the sense of a flower unfolding, revealing more and more meaning the deeper we examine it. For that reason, for example, it usually takes far more words in prose to express the meaning of a poem than the poem itself used, and frequently, even after our best attempts, the poem still evades absolute explication.

Compression—the art of saying much with little—is fundamental to effective poetry. From haiku, which consciously avoid unnecessary words and concentrate on every sound and syllable, to longer, more expansive pieces, poetry struggles to expand beyond mere word count. And one of the most common difficulties a poem encounters is the sense on the reader's part that it is wordy, bulky, flabby.

As a matter of practical application, there are two large divisions of words in English: structure words and lexical words. *Structure* words function primarily as adjuncts of syntax and grammar. They do not carry significant meaning in themselves but instead provide important signals as to how other words relate to each other and to meaning. They are notoriously difficult to define specifically; most often, definitions tend toward the abstract. The simple preposition *for*, for example, can mean "with the object or purpose of," "intended to belong to or used in conjunction with," "in place of," "to the amount of or extent of," and literally dozens of other possibilities; its specific meaning in a given phrase depends entirely on the meanings of the words that surround it. In general, structure words include prepositions, articles (*a, an, the*), and the copular verbs (*is, seems, becomes*, etc).

Lexical words, on the other hand, can be defined. They relate to specific things, actions, movements, qualities. Their meanings usually refer to image-making constructs: *walk, run, touch, tree, fence, boulder*. In most cases, these words are nouns, verbs, adjectives, and adverbs.

> [CAVEAT: At this point it is important to emphasize that there is nothing inherently **wrong** with structure words, or with using them within poetry; nor does the presence of lexical words automatically make for tight, lean, effective lines. Structure words do, however, frequently occur unnecessarily and add bulk, a sense of the prosaic, and a rhythmical flatness when not used carefully and consciously, just as lexical words can create a sense of vividness, imagery, action, and specificity.]

Let's begin by looking at the most notorious of the structure words: prepositions.

One on-line dictionary defines *preposition* as "any member of a class of words found in many languages that are used before nouns, pronouns, or other substantives to form phrases functioning as modifiers of verbs, nouns, or adjectives, and that typically express a spatial, temporal, or other relationship, as in, on, by, to, since." The definition is long, abstract, and cumbersome, particularly since the words being categorized tend to be remarkably short and direct. For practical purposes, however, perhaps the best definition of a preposition is "anything a rabbit can do to a hill": in the hill, on the hill, by the hill, around the hill, through the hill. Only a limited number of words function as prepositions in English, yet at the same time they are among the most difficult class of words to use idiomatically and "correctly." In spite of all this, they are essential to creating meaning in English.

In terms of compression, however, prepositions almost always add words, often unnecessary words. By definition, a *pre*-position comes before something; therefore prepositions, when functioning as such, always have objects, words that function as nouns. These, in turn, are frequently prefaced by articles (*a, an, the*) which in essence simply announce "Watch out! Noun coming."

Three words. Only one carrying meaning.

Let's look at an example from one of my earliest poems, an elegy to my uncle:

> For in the soothing sounds of waters' whisperings
> As they turn a moss-encrusted wheel,
> He is present.

Ignoring other problems for the moment, look at the first two lines. Fifteen words—three prepositions (*for, in, of*), two articles (*the, a*), a vague pronoun (*they*), and a wasted adverb (*as*). Nearly half of the total devoted to telling readers how words—substantive, meaningful words—fit together or relate to each other. And the poor reader has to make it to the fourth word before anything is actually said. An overly long, bulk, uninteresting set of lines.

To revise for compression and energy, let's first look for a verb. The sentence, as written, has one, of course: *is*, the weakest verb in English (more about that in Part III). In addition, it comes so late in the lines that the reader has to perform a juggling act just to keep all of the intervening parts straight.

If we look for an active verb—or a word that could become an active verb—a couple of things emerge. First, words such as *soothe, sound, whisperings* and *turn* could easily become verbs. And second, the sentence as it stands makes no sense; stripped of verbiage, the opening clause actually reads, "sounds turn a wheel"—not at all what I was trying for. Wordiness, precipitated by incessant prepositions, gets in the way of meaning.

So...in that opening clause, where is our true verb? Probably the most likely is the noun *whisperings*—rather artificially nominal, since if we remove the noun-making endings, we get a strong verb: *whisper*. What whispers? *water*. Where? *through a moss-encrusted wheel*. And we have a sentence: "Water whispers through a moss-encrusted wheel."

But we have more than that. What happened to "sounds?" In its noun form, *whisper* is a sound; the earlier, more abstract, more general (how many kinds of sound are there?) word is redundant. What about "soothing"? Don't whispers usually soothe unless otherwise described, especially in an elegy? And if water whispers through a waterwheel, doesn't it turn the wheel?

In essence "Water whispers through a moss-encrusted wheel" says everything implicit in the first two lines, using seven words instead of fifteen, one preposition instead of three, and eliminating "they" and "the."

What, then, to do with line three, which asserts bluntly the point of the image: "he is present." Again, *is*, the weakest of verbs, followed by *present*—vague, abstract, generalized, non-imagistic, boring. The only word truly working here is *he*, which in the context points specifically to an individual: my uncle. Three more words (bringing the total to eighteen); only one carries significance for the lines.

This brings us back to an earlier problem: what do these lines want to say? When I wrote them, I was standing beside a waterwheel my uncle had built perhaps forty years earlier, moss-encrusted as the line says, still functioning. Just seeing it, hearing it, brought him forcibly back to memory. So what should the subject of these lines be? *Water*, which seems at this point tangential; or *he*? Let's go with the latter. If we move *water* to a different place in the line, and replace *a* with *his*, we get:

> He whispers through his moss-encrusted waterwheel.

More imagistic, metaphorical, possibly symbolic, certainly more interesting—in seven words, fewer than half of the original count but saying more clearly what I intended.

Are we finished? Perhaps. A judicious break might transform the line into creditable free verse:

> He whispers through
>   His moss-encrusted waterwheel.

Or we could keep going, transforming and re-structuring:

> His moss-encrusted waterwheel whispers…*him*.

Possibly simply:

> His moss-encrusted waterwheel whispers….

Or transform it into a haiku-like sequence:

> moss-encrusted
> waterwheel—
> his ghost whispers

Or any number of other possibilities, none readily apparent in the first version.

Of all the parts of speech, then, prepositions (and their accompanying nominal phrases) most often work against tightness, compression, and clarity in poetry. Lines needn't be stripped down as far as I have taken this one, but on almost every level, particularly in early drafts, finding prepositions and prepositional phrases, identifying the underlying verb, defining the actor performing that action, and restructuring accordingly may at least present new alternatives for expression.

EXERCISES

10. METRICAL VERSE

(a). Write a poem of at least four quatrains using a regular meter *other than* iambic tetrameter or iambic pentameter. At the bottom of the page, identify the meter you selected. Use one of these rhyme schemes:
   ABAB BCBC CDCD DEDE
   ABAB CDCD EFEF GHGH
   ABBA BCCB CDDC DEED
   ABCB BCDC CDED EFEA
Also indicate whether you are using full or slant rhyme, or some other variation on rhyme (analytic, concept, etc.)

AND

(b). Write an English [Shakespearean], Petrarchan, Spenserian, Miltonic, or other traditional variation on the fourteen-line, iambic pentameter sonnet. Possible rhyme schemes:
   ABAB CDCD EFEF GG
   ABBA CDDC EFFE GG
   ABBAABBA CDECDE

Examples:
   George Herbert, "Prayer (I)"
   Gerard Manley Hopkins, "Pied Beauty"
   William Butler Yeats, "Leda and the Swan"
   W. H. Auden, from "Five Songs"

William Shakespeare, SONNET 73

That time of year thou mayst in me behold
When yellow leaves, or none, or few do hang
Upon those boughs which shake against the cold
Bare ruin'd choirs where late the sweet birds sang.

In me thou see'st the twilight of such day
As after sunset fadeth in the west,
Which by and by black night doth take away,
Death's second self, that seals up all in rest.
In me thou seest the glowing of such fire
That on the ashes of his youth doth lie,
As the death-bed whereon it must expire,
Consumed with that which it was nourished by.
This thou perceiv'st which makes thy love more strong,
To love that well which thou must leave ere long.

DEATH ON A DIRT-ROAD HIGHWAY

"Just a flat," they said, "it was just a flat."
It killed that unnamed man on the Rimrocks
One July noon when heat-waves seemed to float
In ripples over deep-scored tire-scarred ruts;
I can imagine him driving westward,
Rattling in a decade-old forties' coupe,
Bald tires *hummm*ing, spitting gravel toward
Home, then *thumpthumpthump* as something sharp cut.
The coupe stuttered still. He removed the tire,
Felt for sharpnesses protruding inside,
Sliced his thumb as poison-flooding fangs tore
Flesh as easily as rubber. He died.
Today, a twisted branch in predawn light
Seemed a fangless rattler. My breath stole flight.

PLAYING "THE LOST CHORD"

It's a solo for organ by Arthur himself,
With no touch of Gilbertian patter—
Since no one has heard it in twenty long years,
If I make a mistake it won't matter.

I pull out the stops, the low and the high,
I brace up the music, and pray—
Then take a deep breath, check once at my feet,

Press down with four limbs…and I play!

The organ resounds with inimitable sounds—
Principals, strong diapasons…
I'm lost in the notes. Ward members sit still—
And for once I don't care if I'm playsome.

I begin with the lightest of possible flutes,
Transmuted to strong piping breaths;
But halfway along the music transforms
To the pedal Posaune's sharp depths.

I thunder and rumble through chord after chord;
I glory in rapturous sound,
Then stop…hear the echo of silence divine,
And the Chord that was lost has been found.

FALLEN FAIRY TALES

As the music starts playing she runs for the truck,
With her eyes wide and gleaming, her feet racing fast.
But the truck takes a turn and it cruised right past,
As she yells for her mother to give her a buck.

So the kids head for home, and she finishes last,
And then bolts up the steps and flings open the door.
But her mom hands her money (like never before)
So she flies out the door as it slams with a blast.

When she reaches the truck she begins to adore
All the flavors of ice cream that she's never tried,
But she chooses the pink kind; vanilla inside.
As she takes her first taste, the cone falls to the floor.

And she brings up her hand over tears she can't hide,
But she wipes them and turns from the syrupy mess
And looks down at the spot on the front of her dress,

Knowing well that dad's ice cream man fairy tale lied.

MARKET DAY, ON SUNDAY, OR ANY DAY

Sought by cannibals and concubines,
A pruned old Mayan woman ambled down
The cobblestone, to sell her knowledge. Brown
Arthritic feet stopped at a rot-wood shrine.

Worn faces gathered in the square for prayer
And profit, set up shop as morning bells
Began their rhythmic clamor. A priest sells
Them faith. A soldier paces. They prepare

To vend their weaved goods, plastic toys, some jade
Their silver, souls, meat. Tourists run amuck
Watched by yellowed monster angels, stuck
To crumbling Spanish bell towers, afraid.

In time with morning bells begins the beat
Of automatic weapons down the street

SNAKE OIL

Speak sharp with your steel tongue
Pull me down the pit to
Rank rot and the
Shout zoo

Flies fade in your hoarse hue
Snare and flare me blindly
Deep down with a
Cocked key

Stop swift at the thorn tree
Tie my hands and find a
Soft seat as my
Flesh frays

Smile spreads when my eyes die
Satisfied -- savor
Sweet drops to dry,
Tight tongue

> [I used trimeter, dimeter, and monometer and a combination of spondees, phyrrics, trochees in the following metric pattern: // uu //, /u /u /u, // uu, //.]

CREEKROCK

creekrock sleek-rock ticking geoLogic
time   cold-moss-hung clock-intrusion fractured
cutting/jutting/rutting iced-magmatic
tears glacial tears condensed coarse-crystal hard-

ness   thrusting/bursting/thirsting   melting heat
compression into quartz   feldspar [pink-white
plagioclase sheer orthoclase] grain-grat-
ing crush crystal into crystal into light

softness melts hardness endures inures it-
self to aeons   weight pressure heat   heat
pressure weight   and shatters with unending bite
ice snow wind heat snow Wind Ice TIME   abate

weight   thick-sediment-clothing slides away
creekrock glistens moistens   enlightens day

A PALL-BEARER AT A FEBRUARY FUNERAL

Peaceful day, no pain or trouble
Mother calls and kills my pleasure
Grieving time I knew would come
Nothing stops one's death from cancer

Anguish starts I cannot measure

Touching cheeks that feel so numb
Eyes are fastened, viewing nothing
Watching where I cannot fathom

Heart, a pounding, beating drum
Winter leaves are cracking, rustling
Oak is clutched in frigid hands
Feet that lead me stagger, slowing

Lie him here in native lands
Dwelling now in God's embrace
That is what the soul demands
Once returned to earthly rubble

[Meter is trochaic tetrameter]

WHEN SPRING UNFURLS

When Spring unfurls from showers' mist in May,
And mountains swelling mudelicious, green
Beneath the fresh sun light, and flowers glean
A paisley palette dancing in the sway

As curling breezes wash the sprouting hills,
And budding fruitrees spout emeralds leaves
From turgid branches, and the busy bees
Alight on blossoms blooming, bussing fills

The air with hollow hums, and butterflies
Ballet on whisping breaths of perfumed air,
And feathered fauna flutter, chirping fair
Melodies as they swing through azure skies;

As the dew's last drip drops and sprinkles flee,
Upon that dappled hillside you'll find me.

BONUS EXERCISE

Explore the possibilities of non-traditional sonnets by writing in an alternative forms. You might try a blank verse sonnet (meter but no rhyme), a slant rhyme sonnet, a tetrameter sonnet, a free verse sonnet (first considering carefully how such a thing might look), a diminishing sonnet (in which each quatrain/couplet is one foot or one syllable shorter than the preceding one), a sonette (half sonnet, iambic pentameter, rhyming *abba cbc*), or any other variations you might discover.

IN A TIME OF LOSS: SONETTE

The time of iris closes slowly, still.
One day they flourish, glossy, fragrant, proud
Behind my home, a vibrant rainbow-cloud—
Flags, varicolored, serried on the hill;

Then gone. A day, no more, and petals twist
To parchment brown, a sullen summer-shroud—
Until next springtime blooms, they will be missed.

107°: DIMINISHING SONNET

With summer comes the triple-digit heat,
Its stultifying swell of mercury
Wavering walls that—merciless—thrum and beat
Road-asphalt into softened anarchy;

With heat comes lethargy, long seconds
Without a breath, it seems, undying,
As if an endless moment beckons,
Withdraws, attenuates, sighing;

And lethargy devolves to dearth—
No energy, no will, no life
Beyond hard-baked and stolid earth,
Devoid of vigor or of strife;

Consumed by fire's caress,
All seems motionless.

THOUGHTS ON A SUNLIT DAY IN FEBRUARY: BLANK-VERSE SONNET

Past snows are just furled memories, except
For grey-stained slits that linger (solemn hints
Of what may be yet to come) in shadowed
Coolness near dim, northern sides of houses.

The lawns lie barren, brown, no hints of green
Yet shattering stiff shrouds of winter-death,
No wild, luxuriant softness beneath my
Feet as I cross to check for half-feared mail.

Irises lay buried in tangled mats
Of last-year's spear-sharp leaves, unwittingly
Reminding in their desolation of
Promises only April warmth can meet.

And thus. Brightness tinged with ambiguous
Chill—dreariness suffused with latent light.

11. REVISION II

Revise one poem written as part of these exercises. You *must* change the form and in a paragraph following the poem identify how the change strengthened the poem.

Example 1:

BLUEBOTTLES CRUST WITH DUST [original]

Bluebottles crust with dust
On window ledges long
Since scrubbed and painted—just
As once they did a life
Ago, when attic must
Drew an iron filing
With its magnetic lust.

BLUEBOTTLE FLY [revision 1]

With a grey, heavy *hmmmmm,* a fly
Again attacks the window's dust-baked pane;
Its mica-wings, two gyrous blades,
Distress the attic's stale air to feign
A rush of breath.

Tik-thump! Its glossy weight abuts
Rippled glass so ancient the apple tree
Abrading the splintered sill curves cut
With fracture lines distorting bud and leaf
In purling death.

I slip the lock into the jamb
And tiptoe backward down must-laden stairs;
That heavy, grey *hmmmm* vibrates
My fear, becomes a dirge-song in my ear,
A pain-pent breath.

An hour. Two. Three. I

Unslip the lock and shiver through the door.
The fly lay dead, its corpse a scrawl
Of dust in dust, its *hummm* a fading spoor
Of echoing death.

BLUEBOTTLE FLIES—

> SENTINEL IN GRANDMA'S ATTIC [revision 2]

With grey and heavy *hmmmmm*s, a fly again
attacks the window's dust-baked pane; its wings,
two gyrous blades, distress stale air to feign
a rush of breath. *Tik-thump!* Glossy weight

bows rippled glass, and ancient apple trees
abrading splintered sills curve shadows, cut
thin fracture lines distorting buds and leaves
to knit-purl death. I slip the ancient lock

to jamb, tiptoe backward down dust-graven
stairs. That grey-toned *hmmmm* becomes a sudden
pain-pent breath. I wait. Unslip the lock. Shiver
past the door. The fly—a scrawl of dust in

Dust. Along the ledge, bluebottles crust—
Black filings flung to time's magnetic lust.

Example 2:

FETE [original]

Dew forms silver apples on marbled quartz tiles, fragile
crystal goblets sit awaiting
masked humanity—
parasols
aside
for
now.

MEDITATION ON RE-DISCOVERY [revision]

Dew forms silver apples on marbled quartz tiles, fragile stick
crystal goblets bend with wind;
nocturnal essence--

Perfumed beads of glass on flesh chills bare curved neck which,
from gods' breath, hangs on silk breasts;
icicle bells sing--

Notes tickle inside whisper-soft elf ears covered in
glistening sweetrain droplets;
velvet sensation--

Cream colored flavors layer tongues ravenous, viscous,
honeyed, gratifying hunger;
approaching near-bliss--

Feathery voluminous cotton-clouds pass under
hands curious, untainted.
I, satiated.

> [This poem started out as a Fibonnacci, but I chose to change it into syllabic verse. I really liked my first line and wanted to continue with the "dreamlike" quality. I feel that lengthening the poem into 15 lines, while using the syllabics as a organizational form significantly increased the effectiveness of the poem.]

Example 3:

LOVE AT FIRST SIGHT [original]

Sitting on a park bench
reading Dean Koontz's *Watchers*,
she unknowingly entered

my life as I noticed her long,
dark, wavy hair swaying with
the gentle breeze that
peacefully calmed the warm summer
day when love at first sight
became more than just a trite
phrase as I innocently passed
by her our eyes met in a
breath-taking stare and our souls
were as one for that brief moment.

NEVER [revision]

Never:
have we made passionate love
by the soothing ecstasy of the
fire place as the flames dance,

shared an intimate kiss while
the sun sets splashing brilliant
shades across the animated sky,

embraced in each others tender arms
under the crescent moon when the
waves gently fall blowing a cool breeze.

Yet:
for that single brief moment our
eyes met in a trancing stare and
seduced our souls fused together as
one.

> [In writing this revision, I tried to take an idea and express the same message in the second poem that was expressed in the first. I tried to enhance the description of the second poem from that of the first. Also the

first poem was made from an exercise in the Creating Poetry book, which was to make a poem in entirely one sentence. The second poem was more structured in its writing where I was using the lines to help enhance the strength of the poem.]

12. Villanelle

The villanelle has a basic line of either iambic pentameter or tetrameter. The first five stanzas are tercets and the sixth is a quatrain. The poem is constructed on two rhyme sounds, with stanzas linked by rhyme pattern and repeated lines. The first line of the poem recurs as the last line of stanzas two and four; the third line recurs as the last line of stanzas three and five; and the first and third lines form the concluding couplet of stanza six. The rhyme may be diagrammed as follows:

A^1 b A^2
a b A^1
a b A^2
a b A^1
a b A^2
a b A^1 A^2

Form: iambic pentameter/tetrameter.

Examples: Dylan Thomas, "Do Not Go Gentle into that Good Night" [*TBAP* 631]

THE STALKER'S PROMISE

Now I have seen your calmness. Shake and crack
As you might wish it too, I have seen.
I promised yesterday I would come back

To visit you, to give you what you lack
Of love and passion's haunting lore. I've been
Where I could see your calmness shake and crack

Like cliff sides after torrent-rains, where mud-black
Flows engulf whatever stands between.
I promised yesterday I would come back,

And I shall come, no fear, I know the knack

Of subtlety in what you say and mean.
Now I have seen your calmness shake and crack,

And sense better than you see yourself the wrack
Of unanswered heat that will be…that has been.
When I promised yesterday I would come back

You whispered 'no,' your nails tore a track
Of blood, a caustic fragrance coppery keen.
But I have seen your calmness shake and crack;
I promised yesterday…I will come back.

LESTAT IN DRAG

She never once cared to see his face—
He held the precious fluid.
The darkened club, a perfect place

to approach and seduce a sweet kiss, trace
his fine throat with lips raw, red—
she never once cared to see his face.

The heart began its familiar pace,
rushing blood in veins calm, un-dead—
the darkened corner, her chosen place;

and when he trusts most, then embrace
and devour, ravage, drink—be fed.
She never once cared to see his face,

she had to feed The Hunger, taste
it—that to which her body owes debt—
the dark floor, his resting place,

a piece of naive prey. She leaves no trace
behind of her urgent feast and
never once cared to see his face;

the darkened club was a perfect place.

THE PRESENCE

There's something in the presence of a child
That puts an end to dark thoughts' stark travail—
It soothes the turmoil when my heart runs wild;

When all about me seem to have reviled
Without a word, and confidence grows frail,
There's something in the presence of a child.

When custom has my willing soul beguiled
To thoughts of emptiness beyond the pale,
It soothes the turmoil. When my heart runs wild

And echoing recriminations piled
Against the self warn that it might fail,
There's something in the presence of a child.

When friendships ache as if to tendrils filed
By loss, and shadow threatens to prevail,
It soothes the turmoil when my heart runs wild;

It takes so little. A fragment glance, a mild
Remark, a gesture lost in small detail….
There's something in the presence of a child;
It soothes the turmoil when my heart runs wild.

THERE ARE CERTAIN THINGS WHICH FOLLOW A CURVE

There are certain things which follow a curve
And bend with force or ease the rigid line
Inward, inward, past the nets of nerve.

The folding hills now green now brown endure,
The subtle concave waves of sea, define

The certain things which always follow a curve.

They arch their backs into a question and serve
To turn the bulging bloodshot eye of Time
Inward, inward, past the nets of nerve.

Our palmed hands of parenthesis preserve
The memories of this twisted vine—
There are certain things which follow a curve.

They lie beyond the layered bricks of words
Where dark and soiled rivers run serpentine
Inward, inward, past the nets of nerve.

Our bodies, rolling smooth and round infer
A tenderness where shape and thought entwine—
(There are certain things which follow a curve,
Inward, inward, past the nets of nerve.)
—Christian Hawkey
Award Winner, 1992 *Poet* competition

MOVING WITHOUT SIGHT

I stumble, hands out, moving without sight,
And pass through streetways, unsure where to go.
I long for guidance; need to feel his might.

Each day I take a steadfast step with fright,
And wish someone would harness me in tow.
I stumble, hands out, moving without sight.

Each turn I make is blind, as if in night.
Though scared, I run, afraid to take it slow.
I long for guidance, need to feel his might.

Adrift at sea, no guide map for my flight,
I hope for currents' planned, directing flow.

I stumble, hands out, moving without sight.

I choose my way, though I don't feel the light,
Or gardener's hand to plant and watch me grow.
I long for guidance, need to feel his might.

I look around and search for what is right,
believing truth, but who's truth I don't know.
I stumble, hands out, moving without sight,
And long for guidance, need to feel his might.

GERRY

I hated working with Gerry
at Riggin's Cattlemen's Restaurant.
It was weird and even scary.

I'm King, Master Culinary
waving deadly knives he'd taunt.
I hated working with Gerry

alone with no intermediary
to prevent a fun abducting jaunt.
It was weird and even scary.

Them bloody hands ain't sanitary
touching steaks—fingers red and gaunt.
I hated working with Gerry

who even asked me to marry
him with a fake ring to flaunt.
It was weird and even scary.

I'd be the bride of the cemetery
and live—a homely cafe haunt.
I hated working with Gerry
It was weird and even scary.

13. SESTINA

A French syllabic form with six sestets and a final tercet (the *envoi*). The stanzas repeat six terminal words in a fixed order: *abcdef faebdc cfdabe ecbfad deacfb bdfeca*. The *envoi* uses a terminal word in the middle and at the end of each line, arranging them *be dc fa* or *be cd fa*.

Examples:
Arnaut Daniel, "Sestina" [*TBAP* 600-60; Drury 253-254]
Elizabeth Bishop, "Sestina" [Drury 254-255]

IDAHO SESTINA

Beyond swirled, time-worn crests of sage—
Grey-grey outcasts in the shade of Chimney Rock—
Stretch Elba's sheltered, hedge-quartered fields.
To the south, the ragged gash of Hollow Creek
Etches aspen-burnished mountain flanks coiled above farms
That meander north toward the Albion Road.

Gravel-strewn, the scimitar curve of Albion Road
Severs narrow arteries of pungent sage,
Then cuts the western edge of Grandpa's farm
Near where it lies silent beneath Chimney Rock,
Near where the algae-gutted basin that was once Hollow Creek
Widens to irrigate dry-golden fields.

Once hard red winter wheat bearded the fields,
Whiskered the eastern edge of old Albion Road
And curled across the valley to the mouth of Hollow Creek;
Once one-room cabins nested in cups edged with sage
And rode the slopes across from Chimney Rock—
Once, when Great-great-grandpa settled here to farm.

For decades now, no new folk have come to farm;
They buy the red brick houses...but ignore wide fields

Lying fallow and neglected in the scowl of Chimney Rock;
They guide slick RV trailers along the curve of Albion Road
Where horse-drawn wagons rattled through thick sage
On their way to picnics up Hollow Creek.

It's been years since people drove the rocky road up Hollow
    Creek;
Years since fields were sown on Grandpa's farm;
And what was garden then…now repossessed by sage
And sego lilies and russet paintbrush dotting fields
That lie alien and cold against the curve of Albion Road,
Beneath the jutting snaggletooth of Chimney Rock.

No one nowadays notices Chimney Rock,
A lonely sentinel gazing stonily up Hollow Creek
From vacant height above the new-paved Albion Road;
In the valley, shadows leap from farm to dying farm,
Scatter twilight darkness like seeds upon dead fields—
Wombs of bone-white, weaving sage.

He drives beneath Chimney Rock and looks across the farm,
Winds up Hollow Creek, and tromps through new-mown fields—
In memory. Albion Road bisects grey-green shades of sage.

THE CASKET

From her window, I remember following a parade of black
ghosts drifting towards the oakwood casket; tears flowed through
the aisle, soaking my vinyl shoes and drenching hand-
kerchiefs held by familiar faces. We sat near the cross,
which guarded the casket, kneeled, and bowed heads.
I never saw his eyes dark and wet. At morning time,

he would greet me with sun-kissed eyes. Time-
sands - rough and coarse - seeped through the deep, black
hole, then scattered in his heart. Thunder pounded his head
and clouds cast across his lids. Heaven's light penetrated through

the stain-glass, blessed her casket, and the monstrous cross
grew taller and wider. Veins protruded her fragile hands,

which once cradled me to sleep. I watched a hand-
some man drop to his knees wailing, "It wasn't her time
to go! It wasn't her time!" Staring at the casket, I crossed
my arms, shivering at the dead angel. Everything turned black
in my mind. Face was coated with color wax, but through
the eyes of a child, she was a beauty. Her head

rested on a satin pillow with white fringes. At the head
of the casket, white roses surrounded her. My hands
reached for her, but fear pulled me back. Again, he threw
his arms across her and wailed, "It wasn't her time
to go!" She was a Sleeping Beauty with her jet black
hair and ruby lips. We made the sign of the cross,

and kneeled. The priest read the Bible and I looked across
His House, staring into the deadened eyes and cowered heads
of loved ones. The casket slowly closed and black-
ness fell across her body. He touched my hair and I felt a hand-
ful of tears fall down my hair and face. In time,
I learned about that day and all he went through.

Now, stars sprinkle their dust on my head like his tears. And from
her window, I remember. A faint gust of wind crosses
my heart, pushing the memories behind. Time
never heals; it buries pain in a sacred place we later head
to. But, I still remember her ruby lips kissing my hand;
kissing his lips. And I remember her jet black

hair flowing through her veil, her head
resting near the cross, his big hands
holding mine, and that time - seeing black.

FOUR SEASONS

Then April springs from cloudless sky,
Leaping to and fro on leaves
Of grass blown by birthing breezes.
Kaleidoscope flowers paint
A Pollack splattered canvass. The air,
perfume pregnant, swirls crisp,

Sweeping dandelion seedpods from crisp
Stalks and swings them whimsically sky-
Ward. Spring subsides. Then August air
Hangs heavy, stifling, and browned leaves
Scuttle the knolls with muddied paint.
The scaling, dryness of stagnant breezes

Burns your nostrils. Rarefied breezes
Quiver with chalkboard scratches as crisp,
Cracked blades rustle in the paint-
Peeling heat. The yellow sky,
Sun filled and silent, chars leaves
Before dissolving in the saunalike air.

Then November falls from summer's air
With cold, condensation filled breezes
From an open refrigerator door. Fireleaves
Ignite the Sycamores and fall crisp,
Brittle. The graying, overcast sky
Hangs over orange and red paint

Stippled ground. Colorless paint
Drips from closing clouds and the air
Smells thick with dust. A seamless sky
Darkens in December as icy breezes
Whip through barren trees. Crisp,
Crackle-crust dusting leaves

A fleecy snowcoat covering leaves,
Fallen in Fall, with white paint-
Like powder paste. Morning's crisp,
Clean, cold, cutting air
Blows in unforgiving breezes
Below the lead colored sky.

Then ice leaves and March air
Returns with painted hills, and breezes
Wipe the crisp, cloudful sky.

THE PENGUIN CAFE

(open 24 hours)

Tuesday. Two A.M. Deserted freeway. I remember the Penguin
and I smile. Craig, Scott, Jeff back when we were all still friends
and Sam and Rich and I could all share
a laugh and a meal together. Now, the airports
have pulled us apart leaving me to pick
up odd jobs in Los Angeles and look for cheap

rent. God. We used to go there, at first because it was just cheap.
A burger for $3. Fries 50 cents. But the Penguin
had more - omelettes, deli sandwiches, reubens, meatloaf, take
          your pick!
You always chose between two good things. Friends
loved it. Anyone you took there, often en route to the airport,
couldn't help but feel the ambiance - something to share.

And when you had stuffed yourself, you still *had* to share
dessert - garbage can cookies and ice cream. Pretty cheap
when you consider it took four guys to eat it. Any airport
ride was preceded or followed by a stop at the Penguin.
Pay off for driving. All our friends
knew and they always offered. "Just pick

me up early. Penguin Run." Gumballs, Cologne machine,
    toothpick.
Traditions. Mark always had a Lime Rickey. Chris an Egg
    Creme. Me, Cherry
Coke. I was always first to the jukebox. My friends
would roll their eyes as I punched up James Brown. Cheap -
2 songs for 25 cents. 'Take the A Train.' 'Rockin Robin (Tweet).'
    The Penguin
sign read "Open 24 Hours;" music played to drown out the airport

sounds. But even if you didn't have to hit the airport,
you always dropped by. Kick back. Shoot shit. Pick
on the cute, I mean cute high school girls who worked at the
    Penguin.
They smiled. They blushed. And if they *liked* you, your bill
    shared
the black plastic tray with not one, but ten pieces of cheap
bubble gum. Bazooka. Bazooka Joe. (laughter) Me and my
    friends

always wanted to, not jump her, not slap an ass, just give her a
    kiss. Friendly,
innocent, adorable. We fell in love, right by the airport
in black and white tile rooms. Black tie. White hat. Black mini-
    skirt. White socks. Nothing cheap
about it either. The stoic Mexican cooks pick-
ing around in the kitchen never said a word, yet seemed to share
from behind the red oatmeal boxes, flour tins, corn flakes, our love
    of the Penguin.

The last time, November, we three friends would be together, Fate
    picked
a sorry time for our goodbyes. Before the airport, he, she, me
    pulled up and shared
"Clean Teeth." Empty lot. Dark Windows. A cheap orthodontists
    office being built. The lights were out at the Penguin.

ON THE EVENING OF HER 95th YEAR

All that day long, lying still on the rollaway,
   Her head against the soft pillow, not on—
     She cried silently, tears barely visible.
         The room was chilled but she seemed warm
Beneath blue sheets and white eyelet comforter,
     Curled like a child in uneven sleep.

    She was of course no child, no more,
       But her form still barely mounded the
     Bedding. Her talc-white fingers curled
       Once against a soft-starched pillowcase
  When I entered the chilled room, flicked
The light, wiped surprising tears, and spoke.

      She blinked her tears away and coughed,
      Rasping like a child. She trembled
         As if chilled, then sighed against
   The pillow mound—still, silent, lost.
I raised her, her satin-soft arms too thin,
    Too parchment white, with no muscle-weight.

I brought hot soup in a white china bowl,
Age-thinned as translucent tears. I held the spoon.
     She sipped, a soft, blurred sound.
    She paused, lips child-like open, waiting for
More movement in the still, pregnant air,
More warmth against her chilled, tremulant blood.

    I fed her like a child, spoon to lips,
   And held a once-white napkin to her chin
     To sop a spot still glistening on her skin,
Two other spots like tears on her fraying,
Faded nightgown. Child-innocent, she smiled,
And sipped again, a soft and fearful sound.

She ate it all, her soft eyes bright with fever   That made
     her hands more chilled as they brushed
Past mine. With a child's simple weariness
     She rested—white-haired—against my arm,
Speaking nothing, her tears aching as she slumped
     Unbreathing almost, still, and wept her loneliness.

Soft handkerchief lace folded beneath white,
Chilled fingers recalling seventy-two-year-old tears.
Child-mother, she lies—finally—still.

[Note: This poem is an exercise in writing a *medial sestina*, in which all of the repetons (repeated words) occur in the middle of lines rather than at the ends. How effective is this technique? In what ways does it alter the structure, content, and effect of the poem?]

FREE VERSE

Lewis Turco argues that, for various reasons having to do with the accentual structures of French and English, the term *free verse*, as applied to English poetry, is "a misnomer that has clouded the issue for years....one might go so far as to point out that *most free verse poems in English are basically iambic, or mixtures of iambic and anapestic meters*" (*The Book of Forms*). As an alternative definition, he suggests that the term 'free verse' applies primarily to "a line of verse that does not fit into one of the three *metrical* prosodic systems, yet is distinguished from prose by its more emphatic rhythms"—that is predominantly neither *accentual, syllabic,* nor *accentual syllabic*. In general, 'free verse' establishes its basic rhythms through means other than repeated patterns of stressed and unstressed syllables or strict syllable count. Among the possibilities suggested are:

1. **TYPOGRAPHY**—the placement of words to suggest visual patterns that parallel context or content. Typography is linked closely to sound patterns as well. Extreme typographical rhythms may result in **shaped poems** [concrete poems].

2. **SYNTACTICAL RHYTHMS** created by repeating sentence structures and patterns, including **parallel structure, repeated syntactical units,** and **anaphora** (the same words or phrases repeated at the beginning of two or more lines).

3. **SYLLABIC AND BREATH UNITS**—rhythms established by line length. This is the loosest form of free verse, hence the easiest and the one most liable to abuse. Lines break where the reader is expected to breath. The results can be mechanically simplistic; on the other hand, poets such as Charles Olson defend the form because it emphasizes the essentially oral nature of much poetry.

Regardless of which (or what) means you use to create rhythms and unity, the key to effective free verse seems to lie in having a conscious form or pattern for structuring lines—a specific alternative to traditional meter and rhyme. Ineffective free verse often becomes in essence merely prose divided into odd-length lines, frequently without even any recourse to poetic devices—music, repetition, careful lineation—to differentiate it from prose. At the opposite extreme lies the free verse that is essentially metered verse—usually loose iambs—divided again into odd-length lines. Between the two stands true free verse, structured, controlled, conscious, but avoiding overt traditional structures.

14. FREE VERSE—OBJECT

Write a free-verse poem of 15 to 20 lines about a common, concrete object you see every day (i.e., a telephone, a stop sign, a credit card). The poem should depend on imagery rather than on overt philosophy to develop its point. In a paragraph at the bottom, identify the criteria that define line length, rhythm, etc.

Examples:
Henry Reed, "Naming of Parts"
Ted Kooser, "How to Make Rhubarb Wine" [Drury, 130]
Charles Simic, "Fork" [Drury, 181]
May Swenson, "A Navajo Blanket" [Drury 180]

SONATA ENIGMATA

Sometimes the gaping maw—
double-rowed teeth
unsheathed
and ivory white—
frightens me. Is it
grimacing at my pretensions,
subverting my joys

or smiling skull-tight

waiting to consume me
with sound,
chew me thoroughly
and spit out just the hull

PURSUANT TO YOUR REQUEST: "CAN'T YOU WRITE ABOUT SOMETHING BEAUTIFUL, LIKE A DAISY, FOR A CHANGE?"

here lieth a stinking daisy
within weed-ambushed

unclaimed land upon which
some rabid beast or man

prophesied
with his own matter

just one daisy
within a flowery expanse
conforming to natural
dirt deities

wilted
by delicate deformities

a useless thing never tangled
within a young fool's hair nor
arranged to be laid upon
a fresh lovely grave

just crushed
beneath a burden
    of waste and wasted time

SHE JUST WANTED TO TASTE THE WATER

And wandered near the pond.
Wide doe-eyes and swan-neck
descend like feathers, kissing the wind.

She just wanted to taste the water

And caressed the sweet drink
with her tongue, enveloping the liquid
which glides down her throat.

Just wanted to taste the water

And BAM!
Smooth-shaped steel drills her skull,
crushing bones, ripping veins as
blackness rings in her head.

Wanted to taste the water

And dropped as blood masked her face,
warming past thoughts,
dressing her brown coat.

To taste the water.

And breathe as lungs pump steadily, slowly.
Lashes bury eyes, jaws open and
tongue hangs on the pond —

Tasting blood-water.

> [I used *syntactical rhythms* in my free verse poem because of the content of my poem. I repeated the sentence "She just wanted to taste the water" after every 3-line stanza, but I deleted a word each time because I wanted to create the feeling of death. In the deer's mind (person's mind) he/she just wanted to taste the water (or try to get close to someone) and he/she got killed. So, slowly, the deer (person) is dying. Thus, the deer/person isn't able to say a long sentence. Instead, with each last breath, the deer/person is speaking in shorter sentences.
>
> Also, I began each three-line stanza with "And *verb*" to create a rhythm. I placed the repeated sentence on a line by itself to emphasize the innocence of the deer/person: she/he just wanted to have a drink. Also, the repetition of the sentence makes the last line more powerful.
>
> Lastly, I didn't make the line length too long because this poem is about an ordinary incident of a deer near a pond. It's not a long, analytical poem with complex imagery. Thus, I felt that short sentences would create a better atmosphere for the poem.]

ELECTRONIC HABIT

fingers shake, bugs crawl in-
out-through hollow blood-eyes —
c a n ' t   stop —
d r y   shouts
b u r n   *f i x!*
w o n ' t   stop —
pulsing   v e i ns
s n a p   sharp—
m o r e   *juice!*
mind convulses, epileptic Vulcan
hammers a sinewy   sword;
mouth stings, acid-sweat drips
down an arched, arthritic spine,
down crooked, blue-black bone-elbows,
down long nails clawing for crystalline candy.

> [The main structure is concrete. I have added syntactical elements, however, starting most sentences with a noun (a body part), then a condition/state (verb), followed by a sentence with a new noun, a verb, and a prepositional phrase. The monitor is composed of staggered lines, starting with a "can't stop —" or "won't stop —" and followed by an explanation (adj + noun + verb...). Then I parallel the stagger of the keyboard with phrases starting with the word "down." (aside— I've just seen too much of my computer for my own good.)]

THE RECYCLER

We never think of you
Really—until your scent
warns we dump our

cares
worries
sighs

lies

into your ever-waiting
mouth accepting,
without a word

a lone barrette
an old gazzette
a late-night meal
banana peels

once you held
a slighly-stained
red shirt of fleece
and tin cans bathed
in chicken grease

Old Mary hung
them around her
neck
and made
the shirt a hood
for birds to
peck

> [**In the odd breaking of the stanzas I tried to re-create the careless manner in which we throw away what we no longer consider valuable.]

15. FREE VERSE—THREE SUBJECTS

Write a poem to meet *each* of the exercises below. All three poems must be submitted, but identify *one* as superior to the other two.

a. Write a poem of 15-30 lines about eighth grade. The opening lines must refer by name to people you knew then. As the poem progresses, force it to grow beyond autobiography into fiction and image. In a paragraph following the poem, identify how you determined line lengths or rhythm.

AND

b. Write a poem of 15-30 lines about a person or a place you know well. Do not just describe; instead, recreate the *experience* you most fully associate with that person or place. Focus on image, not explanation; show, don't tell. In a paragraph following the poem, identify how you determined line lengths or rhythm.

AND

c. Write poem of 15-30 lines about a color. Again, do not merely describe the color—instead attempt to communicate its essence through senses other than visual, through images other than color. In a paragraph following the poem, identify how you determined line lengths or rhythm.

EIGHTH GRADE

O'Halloran, fat and tall,
Red-wrinkled neck like a dozen
Minnesota winter scarves,
Reeks of laughter and
Punches at the class with his
unlit cigar.

It's three o'clock.
Joey Katts
(Hawk-thin at thirteen)
Disappears into the john,
Blocks the door with his shoulder,
Changes denims for red cotton trunks—
The first to imitate high-school
Football studs who idle by
And jeer through diamond-paned
Cyclone fence. He dares to change
For baseball on the dirt-packed
Diamond, ridges of
Stomach bared and tan
And rippling like ceramic
Tiles.
    I escape O'Halloran early.
Maybe I can sneak into the
John before Joey—and watch him
Strip
And wish I dared.

AT 13,

Julie
frail and frigid
declares herself king of
a pack of rabid girls plodding

through foul pubescent pleasantries
l e t h a l   v i r g i n i t y
dancing topless
locker-

room rows
hellions implode
stomping severely so
serious   bad bad bad babies. . .

pursuing precious sultry skills
less lucid lovers shake
unused hips/wait
some use...

sometime
trembling Julie
chaotic pendulum
pelvis saunters to monkey bars

EIGHTH GRADE REMEMBERED

I was too busy
Perfecting my camouflage
To remember names
Of anonymous assailants
Tripping me on the stairs
Stealing padlocks
Leap-frogging over
As I sat on black-top
Basketball courts
I knew them--
Still know them--
But not by names
Easily forgotten

MABEL GRAFEL

Mabel Grafel—unsmiling, iron-haired,
Grim gargoyle to all fifth-grade rowdies—
Kept rows of violets in neat formations on
A narrow table tucked as if
A lonely afterthought beneath high
Window-banks along the north-most wall of
Burlington School.
                      That winter,
Snow began in January and fell for weeks.

The road to Burlington was graded once a day,
But we small pupils scuttled between iced
Prison walls that towered two feet
Over us as we threaded our long three miles
To the school.
                Everything froze.
Headbolt heaters froze while still
Plugged into engines; sewer lines burst,
Turning whole long blocks of new backyards
Into only slightly fragrant skating rinks—
We ran short PhysEd races on ice-slick walks,
Tucked inside thick fur-lined parkas, and still
Half-froze our lips and noses with each painful
Breath.
         But in *her* room, laid out
In rigid rows upon brown boards that glowed
Rich birch-grain-gold in the angled light,
Her violets prismed winter into spring.

"GRAMS"

Skin soft and sweet
like the most perfect rose petal
and as pale as a fresh
layer of snow.

Her silver mane
shimmers in the sun
like the brightest star.

Blue eyes, clear as
the ocean glistening
under the moonlight.

My guardian angel
on earth, here to
protect me.

Her voice echoes
in my dreams,
she is miraculous.

A SUMMER WALK

No Winter Maintenance, rusts the yellow sign;
the brown road doubles the brown creek,
two firm intentions of unsteady line
that lead the boy between excessive trees
through fleshy smells of leaves and earth in heat,
through bird and insect dither, human silence—
he rounds a curve; his eyes fumble
at a car shoved in a shade
(beyond the next turn,
he hears thunder rumble).
Four legs tumble from the seat,
squirming, spill into the glade;
inside Eve's shorts, he can't see Adam's hand;
he hurries on unknown,
as if to shun a violence:
though not the accident
he'd thought at first,
the sight seemed random
and unplanned as slaughter,
among the rugged certainties of trees,
the furthering, inevitable water
and the sure stones.
The sky repeats its threat of cloudburst;
he hurries home another way.
An image of the pair he's seen
undoes him with unlikely joy;
it throbs his flesh with thoughts
his mind can't mention
as he, brown accidental boy,
wanders in a wilderness of green intention.

FALLEN GOLD CARPET

Fallen gold carpet
Litters the grass
October's Halloween weather
Dark bronzed yellow
Warmer than the fiery sun
Dry leaves crisp as the air
More precious than ore
Smoky wood-smell
I crush them, in my hand
Soft shuffling sound as they slowly fall
While I walk through them

COLOR ME

Scorching stones
Cooled
Warmth rushing, fading
Out your fingers
Leaving feverish evidence
In your memory

Soft hints of heat
Cheeks
In a pinch
Private thoughts
Daringly exposed
In her mind

Taunting youths
Cooked
With blistering rays
Rushing to conform
To fashionable ideals
In their life.

[Note: I wanted the reader to sense the color, rather than see it, yet it was hard not to slip into telling. I feel the last part needs help because I'm telling rather than showing. Line length was made by the poem, not me. I wrote the first stanza in a rush, liked it, worked on it and deciding to model the last two after it.]

GREY

A scintillance of sparrows
spears an old black yew pruned in tough
            triangular grace

beside black asphalt on a bleak
November day—splintering ash
            and charcoal as they

flick the yew with pinions poised, re-
verse, reverse, reverse until they
            blanch white and flat-

sheening feathered mirrors flock grey
clouds, grey sun, grey dying day one
            final burst of light

HOT, SWEATY SUMMER AFTERNOONS

Hot, sweaty, summer afternoons
leave the sky blazing with
protruding colors of the
rainbow.

Overlooking the oceanic scene
the purple haze comes to mind.
A deep, trance-like feeling
fills my body.

In the month of April, dark
violet flowers bloom all
 around me. Reminding me of
my favorite grape kool-aid.

My dark indian colored skin
a purplish color, looks like
I'm freezing, but no goose
bumps.

Unusual transclucent eyes
catch my attention. They
sparkle in the sun and remind
me of her.

> [In this poem I used the same pattern, five stanzas
> showing the images that I think of when I see or think
> about the color purple.]

16. FREE VERSE—THREE THEMES

Write a poem based on each of the following themes:

a. an incident from your childhood or a game you played as a child, using remembered experiences to assess or discuss adulthood;

AND

b. a dream, nightmare, or fantasy, with the imagery of an irrational world used to explore the objective one;

AND

c. other worlds, aliens, or beings beyond your perception—again, not for their own sake but as metaphors for human states.

Identify which of the three seems strongest. The poems may use free verse but must clearly demonstrate rhythmical patterning; they may also be metrical, rhymed, or stanzaic. Your decision on form should reflect the tone and content of the poems. Length: 20-40 lines

WARREN TRAVELS WITH HIS FATHER

in the
dense Montana heat, the BLM vehicle musty
and smelling of oil, sweat, and age.

Warren
skips school for those two days—two days
alone with Dad, staying in old, decaying

motels
where floors feel slick with thin linoleum and windows
glow behind crepe-paper drapes and

single
burner kitchenettes transform outdated army
C-rations into exotic feasts and

lumpy
bedframes support old-fashioned
metal springs that squawk when

Warren's
eighty pounds and Dad's one-eighty
shift. At dawn, they load the truck,

Hunker
down against an early chill, and set out for
the boondocks, Dad to hunt elusive

bench marks
and pace off invisible section lines, Warren to watch
and etch each shifting outline in

his mind,
and store them to relive once they two again
return and reassume their separate lives.

DING DONG

Frantically running
down the block we sped
jumping over fences,
ripping clothed skin on
deadly manzanita,
into strangers backyards
snickering, hiding from our
suspects.

Panting hard we
hung in limbo awaiting safe

signs for recuperation.

Our next target—who knows,
as we regrouped, a school of
hungry pirahnas too powerful
for our bravest adversaries.

Our nest broke up, some moved
married, went to school.
Some just plain disappeared.

Twenty years later, the pounding of
baby calloused feet blistered by
hard cold concrete preys on
our pride filled minds
devoured by bigger fish
as we frantically run door to door
unable to hide anymore, ruining
daydreams we had in school.

> [In this poem, my first stanza is unstructured to give the impression of the rambunctious lives of children playing together. As the poem progresses, the second and fourth stanzas represent inconsistencies with experiences children have as they get older. The third stanza is solidly structured to give the feeling of security children feel in numbers. The fifth standard goes back to life's inconsistencies as the children become adults and no longer possess the security of friends and family. This syllabic approach allowed me to add rhythm to each of my stanzas emphasizing the emotional state of children from childhood to adulthood.]

WORLD GAMES

I told Tommy to don't play with the Big Boys,
But still,

he scurried from our cage, stumbled to the field,
and watched them toss a double-headed coin.
I pulled his brown parka
and he touched my shoulder, telling me to don't worry
Because there's no head hunting in shambattle.

I buried my Levi's in the soil
and when a Big Boy drafted Tommy to be an insider,
Tommy's two silver teeth blinded me.
I stared at Tommy and he glanced my way,
But still,
he hopped onto the field and told me,
"There's no head hunting in shambattle."

From the sideline,
I flinched as clusters of bodies crush and crumble.
Tommy was prey to a tribe of savages.
Slowly,
one by one,
they were eliminated.
But, there's no head hunting in shambattle.

Trigger arms shot a twelve inch bullet.
It flew across the field like the Rocketeer.
The outsiders took turns killing victims,
while Tommy laughed and taunted his foes
Because there's no head hunting in shambattle.

I watched our day's Civil War history lesson come to life
as bodies dropped and soldiers reloaded their guns.
Tommy glanced my way and from the look in his eyes,
I knew that he now understood.
But still,
he continued to dodge the kills.
There's no head hunting in shambattle.

Tommy stood in target zones, while grenades were tossed
and explosives destroyed legs and arms.
He tried to escape, but a Big Boy threw him back to combat.
Tommy brushed the sweat from him forehead -
he looked left,
he looked right -
It was just him.
And them.
The whirring sphere scraped his hair and I yelled,
"There's no head hunting in shambattle!"

I saw a head hunter's burning eyes flame
as Tommy turned his back away from gun.
The hunter fired and the bullet flew towards Tommy.
And before I could scream,
His brains spilled across the field.
There's no head hunting in shambattle.

Tommy's two silver teeth lay in blood and spit.
I knelt next to Tommy and touched his shoulder.
Then,
They took him away
And the Big Boys laughed.
There's no head hunting in shambattle.

> [I used syntactical rhythms and breath units in my poem. I repeated the same phrase in the last line of each stanza to create tension and to give more meaning to the line, "There's no head hunting in shambattle." The stanzas get more and more tense throughout the poem. If you notice, the repeated line has a different effect in each stanza. In the first couple stanzas, "There's no head hunting in shambattle" is just a casual statement or a rule that Tommy makes. But, as we move into the poem, the statement carries a different meaning. In the middle of the poem, the reader wonders if the statement is true because the game becomes more violent. And at the end of the poem, "There's no head hunting in shambattle" is really say-

ing that there is head hunting. I also used breath units to show the readers where to pause because I feel that if the poem isn't read correctly, the overall effect would be lost. (Eg. "But still,")]

HELL

Eerie orange glow,
Gritty smog sunset.
And relentless waves washing
                        ashore, pounding
Savage winds   the shore.
Hurricane froth
From relentless waves washing
                        ashore, pelting
Scorched dunes,   the shore.
Holocaust beach.
And relentless waves washing
                        ashore, beating
Staked to tides,   the shore.
Faceless crucifixion
Amidst relentless waves washing
                        ashore, scraping
                                    the shore.

SIX LETTER M-Y-WORD FOR HAZINESS DREAM

Someone faint is kneeling by the Franklin Stove . . .
Someone faint is roasting pumpkin seeds . . .
Someone faint is rolling tissue into dancers . . .
Someone faint is knitting a wool pull-over . . .
Someone faint is listening to The Shadow . . .
Someone faint is chuckling in the gray rocking chair . . .
Someone faint is checking on whooping Grandma May . . .
Someone faint is lighting a memory candle . . .
Someone faint is holding a worn rosary . . .
Someone faint is fixing a rose to a lapel . . .
Someone faint is finding a six letter m-y-word for haziness . . .

Someone faint is hosting a tea and cucumber sandwich party . . .
Someone faint is smelling African Violets . . .
Someone faint is winding a chiming mantlepiece . . .
Someone faint is wiping off horn-rims . . .
Someone faint is smiling and waving hello . . .
Who is it keeping lockets of hair in the encyclopedia?
Who is it reading the dog-eared Almanac?
Who is it looking through faded albums?
Who is it citing phrases from Song of Songs?
Who is it hiding hand-painted eggs behind sprinklers?
Who is it feeding a parakeet seed from lined hands?
Who is it singing Ave Maria softly in the kitchen?
Who is it waiting patiently for someone faint?

> [I based this on the anaphora form, but I decided that I didn't want to use rhyme because I want to avoid it for now, and also so the poem can show the faint qualities of the form, but it's not quite there . . . I also linked the words by the first two letters and did an abba form, but with the first two letters of the word following the repetition. Also, the last repeating lines are just the letters in order as they appear in the poem a b c d . . . .]

QUESTIONS OF A TYPICAL EXTRA-TERRESTIAL

Every 365 days,
why blow fire
off small sticks
stuck in dark paste?

When earth white,
why set colored boxes
under green tree
ornament laced?

When days long,
why try to shoot

colored stars
to moon?

> [I really wanted to make this rhyme and be very funny. I think that if I had more time and I didn't have such a headache, maybe it would be. I'm sorry I did not finish it, I think I'll try again in my journal because I really like the idea.]

THE WORST KIND OF ALIENS

Barried betwixt behavior...
Hearts
Souls
Dreams.

The worst kind of aliens...
Neighbors
Lovers
Brothers.

Beneath pale, familiar skin...
Green
Blood
Boils.

Cold, acidic liquid flows...
Stagnates
Stranger
Organs.

Heartless creatures hide inside...
Spiradic
Humanized
Lunatics.

17. FREE VERSE— W. GREGORY STEWART IMITATION

Write a poem responding to a poem in the anthology or to W. Gregory Stewart's "Dædalus." You may respond at any level you wish: theme, emotion, context, philosophy, image, structure. Your poem should enter into a dialogue with the original, while at still standing on its own merits. Length: 20-40 lines.

DÆDALUS
    Father, if
        you read this, I am dead,
        a waxen wrack of flesh
        and wing unfeathered. If
    you read this,
        you will know that I
        have tried to touch the sun,
        and you will know that in this
    I have failed.

    But do not grieve,
        my father; do not grieve for me.
        We spent our closest year
        in grand and common dream.
    We gathered quill
        and plume in secret, sought
        the dove for underwing
        and hawk to wrap the winds about
    our farthest reach.

    Finch and eagle,
        eider, too; the every barb
        aligned, reset along its
        shaft, then hidden, placed
    by size and sort

      behind the doors
      behind the doors
      (against the wings
and prying eyes).

And the hives!
      Oh, father, remember the hives?
      Bees robed for comb instead of
      honey were no less angry for that
lesser theft.
      I laid mud upon you and we laughed,
      you as much of earth that day
      as I (too briefly) have been of
the heavens.

Father, I pray
      you, shed no tears for me. Instead,
      a promise: to hold fast that dream.
      Know that it was arrogance—and accident—
but not the dream…
      my own damned fault, perhaps, but it
      was not Apollo cast me down,
      and not the Fates:
they've never cared.

Keep your wings.
      This at the last —if only for
      my memory, cast not your wings away.
      Remember—I have seen the Heavens,
I have flown,
      and having flown would rather be
      as I am not than stricken down
      in dotage, weak and never having
known the sky.

                            —W. Gregory Stewart

RESPONSE POEMS:

PARA PAPI

>Papi,
>>if you see
>
>this,
>smoky, note-filled
>violet rooms and
>shameful, monthly
>welfare checks, you
>did not swallow in
>vain . . .
>
>Papi,
>>if you hear
>
>this,
>eye has failed
>but not the ear,
>that withered over
>worn out wisps of
>melodies always to
>remain . . .
>
>Papi,
>>if you feel
>
>this,
>tremble as I take
>your hands in mine,
>you'll trade your
>pride and drink my
>youth an offer sadly
>lacking . . .
>
>Papi,
>>if you taste
>
>this,

wine, so unlike your
very own, serve it
now with welcomed
wisdom smacking,
like bones your spirit
cracking . . .

TIMES HAVE CHANGED

Oh Levertov, the only thing you know,
is that the stairway is not a thing
of gleaming strands.

Not a stone of glowing optimism
surrounded by a floating flock of angles,
ascending to Utopia.

A gentle sway of wings, no longer
lifts the impressionable man from step to step
on Honest's ladder.

The stairway doesn't exist in the presence
of Darkness' doubt, as they have fused together
in the permeated realm of oneness.

Eroding into a never-ending, downwards
escalator towards Sin's unquenchable
thirst for hate.

With indigestible guilt, civilized human
souls pretend, Evil is merely pondered within
Imagination's darkest corners.

Rather, lurking from shadows,
It lives, grows, takes form, stalks and seduces.
It is too real.

(In response to Denise Levertov's "The Jacob's Ladder")

COMPRESSION II—ELIMINATING UNNECESSARY ARTICLES

Articles fulfill a useful function in English. They serve as placeholders, alerting readers that nouns or noun-functioning words, serving as subject matter for utterances, are coming, if not immediately—as in "the book"—then after an intervening adjective or two—"the red book," "the new red book." They alert us to pay attention. If we miss the noun, we may miss meaning as well. Other kinds of words may also announce nouns, usually possessive pronouns—"my new red book," "your new red book"—or demonstrative pronouns—"this new red book," "that new red book."

Unlike possessives, which indicate ownership or belonging, or demonstratives, which act to point to a specific thing, articles carry little direct meaning. Some nuances are possible. "The" indicates a certain one within an undefined group: "the book"; while "a" indicates an undefined one within an undefined group: "a book," any old book. If the noun begins with a consonant, we use "a"; if it begins with a vowel, we use "an," to make pronunciation easier: "an apron," "an uncle," "an ocean."

[Curiously, the first two words originally began with "n." The earlier middle English forms were "napron" and "nuncle" (preserved as an archaism in Shakespeare's *King Lear*). But gradually the "n" split from the word, slid across the page, and joined the indefinite article "a" to become "an," and our pronunciation and spelling of the words altered accordingly. Fascinating.]

Other languages have different ways of identifying nouns in sentences, usually by specific endings that not only identify a word as a noun but also tell how it functions in the sentence. Some function entirely without articles, allowing these endings alone to signal nouns. Originally, English used such endings—declensions—in much the same way as ancient Latin. The Angle-Saxon word for 'stone' was, for example, *stan*. But a thousand years or so ago, if someone was killed "by means of a" stone, that could be signified, not by a long phrase such as we would have to use, but by a single letter: *stane*.

The point of this for poetry is simply that our ingrained sense that nouns must be preceded by articles can easily spill over into our lines, sometimes creating bulky, unnecessarily wordy poetry. These lines from an early poem of mine seemed, at the time, clear, concise, precise, and artful.

> Watching
> on the fractured rocky shore,
> immersed in misty coolness
> boiling through the heat
> of day,
> he stared into the fog
> as it moved
> in indiscriminate fluffs
> of ragged white
> upon the surface of the lake.
>
> Clouds like darkened petals
> swirling in pools of indigo
> glided through the silences
> between the flowing stars and moon
> and his probing eyes.

I would still argue that, even though they were written a quarter of a century ago, they have a flow, a musicality that I appreciate. However, from the perspective of that quarter-century, I would also argue that they waste a good deal of time in creating poetry.

Combining comments made earlier about prepositions with those above, it might be instructive to simply count instances of structure words in the passage. Boldface indicates preposition, boldface italics indicate articles:

> watching
> **on** *the* fractured rocky shore,
> immersed **in** misty coolness
> boiling **through** *the* heat
> **of** day,

    he stared **into *the*** fog
    as it moved
    in indiscriminate fluffs
    of ragged white
    upon *the* surface **of *the*** lake.

    Clouds like darkened petals
    swirling **in *a*** pool **of** indigo
    glided **through *the*** silences
    between *the* flowing stars and moon
    and his probing eyes.

A casual glance suggests that there are a lot of boldface words. Now for a little mathematics. The passage has 60 words, a nice even number. Of the sixty, eight are articles: *the* (7) and *a* (1)—at least they give the images a slight sense of the specific. Still, 13% of the passage is used primarily to indicate oncoming nouns, most often without intervening adjectives. There are 13 prepositions; 22% of the words primarily indicate relationships between verbs and nouns or between one noun and another.

    Added together, these structure words account for 35% of the entire passage—over one-third of the words do not strictly carry identifiable meaning. And if we add the two conjunctions—*and*—that percentage climbs to 38%. Or conversely, the percentage of words that provide clear action or image amounts to 63%—less than two-thirds.

    This is not to argue that every poem should be subjected to a mathematical counting of parts of speech, or even that all of the occurrences in these lines are weak, ineffective, or problematical. But if poetry is art-with-words, and one purpose of that art is to create image and thereby to stimulate powerful responses within readers, knowing how many words within a poem cannot contribute to either of those ends may prove helpful.

    For the sake of argument, however, let us assume that instead of receiving payment for words (a rare enough event), poets must pay to use words. Clearly, the price exacted for the passage we've just read would be unnecessarily high. So how could we streamline it—concentrating for the moment on articles.

OPTION: ELIMINATION

English is built on embedded principles of redundancy. For example, we immediately recognize *books* as plural because of its final letter; yet it is perfectly proper in English to provide a second, sometimes even more plural-signposts when we use such words. We might say, "I bought six books," or "I bought 300 books"; or more to the point, "**These two** book**s fall** to the floor." For this reason, many non-native speakers, whose first languages may not contain articles or allow such redundancy, might feel quite comfortable eliminating some of the plural markers in the last sentence and simply say "two book fall to floor"—non-idiomatic English but perhaps a literal translation from a native language.

Articles—part of that redundancy—indicate approaching nouns, and we are programmed by conventional usage to include them as often as possible. As poets, however, we can frequently eliminate them without hindering what we wish to say.

Let's look at another line: "The shadow of twilight seemed to outline the tree." Nine words—two articles, one preposition, an infinitive-making *to*, three nouns, and two verbs or quasi-verbs.

With a bit of focus, we can eliminate several words right off. *Twilight* implies *shadow*—we probably don't need both, and of the two *twilight* is more evocative, more specific. *Seemed* as verb is weak; unless there is an underlying sense that what 'seems' really isn't, it wastes syllables. Besides, there is a perfectly useful verb in the sentence already: *outline*.

In one step, we've compressed the line radically. *Twilight* does not usually take an article, so *the* drops out, and we have: "Twilight outlined the tree." Fewer than half the words

OPTION: PLURALS

If we wish, we can remove the remaining article through a simple expedient: English plurals often do not require articles. "Twilight outlined trees." If that seems too bleak, too blunt, we have the option of filling the now-empty noun-placeholder before trees with a more meaningful word: "Twilight outlined dark trees." Four words, all of them carrying meaning.

Then, of course, we could work further, replacing admittedly boring words with more image-forming, more specific, more concrete terms: "Twilight limned stark oaks," or "Twilight brushed weeping willows," or "Twilight scorched saguaros." Or whatever the poem required.

OPTION: MORE SUBSTANTIVE WORDS.
By far the most effective way to deal with excess articles (and the prepositions that frequently accompany them) is to substitute substantive words for the weaker ones. Another example, this time a haiku:

> the light of the moon
> falls upon leafless branches—
> it makes me feel old

Idea: acceptable. Imagery: woefully lacking. Compression: laughable. We have the traditional seventeen syllables; but five of them, nearly one-third the total, are taken up with articles and prepositions. Again, a weak verb: *makes*. And most damning, the poem simple asserts without giving readers an opportunity to enter and imagine.

Now, compression. "The light of the moon" (five words) might become "moonlight." "Falls upon" (weak verb + preposition) could be replaced by a single, more vigorous word, possibly "twists." Now the first line—the first five syllables—might read, "moonlight twists leafless," and we are almost through the second line of the original version.

"Branches" only takes two syllables. If we wish to keep the 5-7-5 structure, we now have five new syllable spaces into which we can place image-forming words. Since all former prepositions have disappeared, let's allow one in at this point…purposefully:

> moonlight twists leafless

> branches into icicles—

Acceptable. But what about that flat final line. Yes, the image might *make* me *feel* old, but neither "makes" nor "feel" works strongly enough now to balance "twists." Keeping the meaning but communicating it through an image, we might get: "fingers rake white hair." And the poem now reads:

> moonlight twists leafless
> branches into icicles—
> fingers rake white hair

Perhaps not a great haiku but certainly far more effective than the original.

> [PLEASE NOTE—even though Part II purports to focus on articles, it is impossible to ignore the fact that frequently multiple articles in a line accompany multiple prepositions; and they, in turn nearly always trigger weak verbs and flat nouns. It is not just a matter of going through a piece and removing or replacing *a*, *an*, or *the*. In most cases, excess articles—and prepositions—merely act as symptoms.]

Now, back to lines I cited earlier:

> Watching
> on the fractured rocky shore,
> immersed in misty coolness
> boiling through the heat
> of day,
> he stared into the fog
> as it moved
> in indiscriminate fluffs
> of ragged white
> upon the surface of the lake.
>
> Clouds like darkened petals

> swirling in pools of indigo
> glided through the silences
> between the flowing stars and moon
> and his probing eyes.

Some possible changes seem obvious: in the lines "glided through the silences/between the flowing stars and moon," both articles can simply drop out, leaving: "glided through silence/between flowing stars and moon" ("silence" sounds better and makes more sense than the earlier plural).

"On the fractured rocky shore" is wordy—and the more interesting and visual noun is not the generalized "shore" but "rock," which has been turned into an adjective. Restore it to its position as a noun, make it plural, and a five-word line (one preposition, one article) becomes a three-word line: "on fractured rocks." That the rocks rest along the shore becomes obvious later, when we see the "surface of the lake."

Perhaps the most enjoyable exercise would be revising these lines:

> he stared into the fog
> as it moved
> in indiscriminate fluffs
> of ragged white
> upon the surface of the lake

which now sound repetitious and bulky. "The fog" requires the next three lines as description. Making "fog" plural would remove the article, but the real problem goes deeper. There are simply too many words, too many prepositions, too many articles for the lines to generate interest.

So…"fog" is white, it cannot appear below the surface of a lake, it is by definition indiscriminate in that its edged are blurred and indistinct. Perhaps all we really need is;

> he stared as
> ragged fluffs curled

>   upon the lake

or something similar. Then, if desired,

>   he watched ragged fluffs curl
>   upon the lake

One benefit of compressing this radically is that doing so forces underlying meanings to surface, to be tested for clarity, logic, precision, accuracy. And then, once we've penetrated the tangle of words, removed deadwood, and structured the poem's core, we can build onto that basic structure as needed/desired and expand through image, metaphor, symbol. Not all poems are skeletal; not all poetic styles can adapt to sparse words/phrases dropping like rocks down the left-hand margin.

But even in more leisurely poems, or in metered poetry where articles and prepositions can function usefully in creating rhythms of stress, challenging, eliminating, transforming, or replacing empty syllables will almost always strengthen the final piece.

EXERCISES

18. CONCRETE POEM

Write a poem in which the physical form of the poem is an integral part of its content and meaning—i.e., a typographical, concrete, found, or otherwise shaped poem.

DOUBLE HELIX

                We
                lie
             face to face
           as if tentative;
      When we sleep we do not know
     but when evening stars begin to glow

    I sleep   *I sleep*
  and stand   *and swirl*
 arching on a bridge   *on grey-cresting waves*
over murky water.   *wind-chipped, cream-curled*
 Mists obscured struts *briar-choked twilit banks,*
  that quivered, hissed. *clouds burned jaundiced*
   I stood afraid   *as I feared*
    and hoped   *and hoped*
     to dream   *to dream*
         to dream

        But   But
     my craft   water roiled
    flowed   soundlessly—
  unobstructed   no pilasters
forever. Midnight   stretched monoliths,
 banks leafmold black no cables, arches,
   meadows cold   fundamental stones—
    and burnt-match only thickened
      brush   air
       alone   alone
        And   And

                              yet
                surging   *bounded*
                  waters   *waters*
                withdrew   *rushed*
              below my bridge.   *toward a bridge*
            Earthbrown waters rushed   *spanning metallic*
            glistening midnight leaves   *thoughts—my coracle*
              first one, two, then   *spun beneath the arch,*
                 the flood   *companion crafts*
                  whirling   *swirling*
                     in   *in*
                  decaying   *fraying*
                         unison
                   I looked   I looked
                upward   downward
                   saw   saw
              his hand reaching   her form radiating
            into muddy mists   terror. Leafmold shot
              and the ironfisted   with greater violence
                undertow writhes   while above
                   my essence in   I plummet to
                    dark water.   dark water.
                          I wake   I wake
                            WE
                           touch
                           engulf
                          become
                             I

THE PHYSICS OF A DYING SUN

```
                            t
               D         h           k
                a
                  o        t
s
                                    u
     i           m       n         n   g
   s   y       a                        b
                  k       o
l
w        i       o       e       e       o
d                        s             a
     h     t     u  They swim, w    m      e
       a              screaming in and out,  s    n
         t    drawn into a thermal melting pot   ?
                    forming ruddy ball which seeks another court,
the wanning light of fire, stretched out into unending shadowed line.
```

PUZZLED SEAS

```
                              but no
                             w at n
                          ight in my absence
          i first    went     he rests unsmiling a
         on a b      oat wi   nd alone.  iron eye
        th father when i had turned si    s in wait
        x. The entire day gripping his s    of my
        mile, even after my nausea un      likely d
            leashe     d on th    elusion. if i became
            e seve     n seas     ailing again possibly
                              he might just move
                                out of t
                                  he way
```

Bonus Exercise

Somewhere between concrete poetry and pastiche lies the **found** poem, in which words are literally 'found' in other sources—newspapers, magazines, other books—and organized by the poet into something new and, in one sense at least, original. Of the various kinds of found poetry possible, one of the more intriguing is the **cento,** in which each *line* of the poem is the opening line of another poem, selected either randomly or by some arbitrary act of choosing, and compiled into a new work of art.

The cento is a fascinating form in that it demonstrates the fluidity of poetic lines, their ability to express more than their literal content, particularly when placed in a new context.

Compile a cento, giving your piece a title that will suggest the organic unity you are attempting to achieve through an overt homage to other poets.

Examples:

CENTO-HAIKU FOR POSTMODERN POETRY

Child of my winter,
    Coming to the cottonwoods—
        Cool black night thru redwoods

[The source poems are: W. D. Snodgrass, from *Heart's Needle*; A. R. Ammons, "Prospecting"; and Alan Ginsberg, "First Party at Ken Kesey's with Hell's Angels"]

IMMUTABLE EYES—
CENTO FOR POETS AND POESY

I am driving; it is dusk; Minnesota—
I am I, old Father Fisheye, that begat the ocean, the worm....

I am not a painter, I am a poet.
I can support it no longer.

I come to tell you that my son is dead—
I do tricks in order to know.

I dreamed last night I dreamed, and in that sleep
I have done it again.

I know if I find you I will have to leave the earth...—
I look out at the white sleet covering the still streets.

> [Source poems: the first ten entries under "I" in the "Index of First Lines," *Contemporary American Poetry,* ed. by Donald Hall, 1962, 1972.]

ODYSSEY I:

FROM THE BACK OF TIME AND FORM

Children are dumb to say how hot the day is,
Everyone agrees.
No sleep. The sultriness pervades the air
To force the pace and never to be still —
Our little tantrum, flushed and misery-hollow.

Cedar and jagged fir —
Earth place —
Nothing, not even fear of punishment
(The flat place of sorrow here)
Opening like a marigold,

Crossing the street.
Each day the time grows less, the hours
Now as I was young and easy under the apple boughs—
Time that is moved by little fidget wheels
On broad hills, the broken backs of mountains.

> [Source: Anagram poem based on entries in the "Index of First Lines," *Broadview Anthology of Poetry,* 1993.]

19. PARODY/PASTICHE

Write a poem that borrows form, content, characters, etc. from a famous work. Usually such poems are comic, but serious pastiches are possible.

Examples:
Arthur Hugh Clough, "The Latest Decalogue"
Anthony Hecht, "The Dover Bitch"; cf. Matthew Arnold, "Dover Beach
Adrienne Rich, "A Valediction Forbidding Mourning" [*TBAP* 746; cf. Donne's poem, p. 42]

ROBO BEN

You can suck Venusian brew
'Til you're plonk and potted, through;
You can try the Martian labels—if you dare!
But when you mine a 'roid,
You will drink the stuff you void,
And be grateful for the fact it's even there.
Now on three-one-four-oh-niner,
Where I used to be a miner
On a seven-year indenture, way back when,
Of all my clanking crew,
The oddest one I knew
Was the wee recycling unit known as Ben.
          It was "Ben! Ben! Ben!
"Is it ready? Well, you'd better hurry, then.
        "Oh, you clatter and you clink
        "But you give me what I drink—
"And I want it now, you rusting Robo Ben!"

Well, he wasn't much to see—
Just a pot for boiling pee,
A flask, some tubing and of course a filter.
Oh, I kept him *well* maintained

As he cleaned the stuff I drained,
For it was hell when he was out of kilter.
He'd roll along behind me
'Til my bladder would remind me
That it was time to handle my affairs.
He'd absorb it like a blotter,
Then produce the purest water—
The answer to a thirsty miner's prayers.
    It was "Ben! Ben! Ben!
 "You pissoir! I am ready once again—
    "Produce me aitch-two-oh, sir,
    "Or it's out the hatch yo go, sir,
 "You uric and mercuric Robo Ben!"

I shan't forget the night
When he wasn't working right,
Consumed by little robo hissy fits.
I was quite consumed by thirst,
But even that was not the worst—
My heating unit went out on the fritz.
I would drip and I would drizzle—
He would sputter and he'd sizzle,
Producing swill that made me wretch and cough.
Well, I lived—though it was hell—
Now I've got my chance to tell
Him, Robo Ben—you really pissed me off!
    So it's "Ben! Ben! Ben!
 "I shall disassemble you, you fiend, and then
    "I shall build machines more tender—
    "Like a toaster and a blender
 "From the parts of that inconstant Robo Ben!"

—W. Gregory Stewart
Parody of Rudyard Kipling, "Gunga Din"

THE PROGRAM

FOR W. GREGORY STEWART AND 'ROBO-BEN'

Once upon a workshift dreary, while I programmed, bleak and bleary,
Stationed at the hard-drive terminal just inside my cubicle door,
While I plodded, nearly napping, there rose a fearful, whirring clacking,
A sound like demons gleefully wracking, racking as in days of yore;
"It's just a glitch," I softly muttered, "just a glitch in the memory core;
> Only that, and nothing more."

Ah, distinctly I remember how, like a distant fading ember,
My server-file refused to send or call my cursor to the fore;
I lost the file I had created, my monitor grew dim and faded,
The malignant-eyed computer made a dismal sputter, just before
It spat one time, then blinked, and then resumed as it had been before.
> It *was* a glitch, and nothing more.

Or so it seemed. But when I called the file I had assiduously hauled
From planetfall to planetfall, defining my parameters for
The requisite restructuring of cells, of blood, of functioning
Anatomy for landfall cloning, cloning tissues as they were;
Then, then!—my God!—the empty spaces that glowed where *I* had been before!
> Only that…and nothing more.

And then I saw the program shifting, each backlit column clearly lifting
External data, clearly sifting through the sentient options. Nor,
With that content, terminating its random matches, random matings

Of gene with gene, recalibrating tissue textures that I wore—
Recalculating planes and tissues in the body that I wore—
                      Changing forms… and something more.

Squint-eyed, peering at the data, poring through white-static strata,
I struggled not to estimate a shape my spirit would abhor;
My fingertips…despairing, flying…praying that the file was lying,
I punched the program, deeply sighing for the peace I'd known before;
"Let it be a disk-drive error," I whispered, damp in every pore:
                      The cursor spelled out: *Nevermore!*"

I stared at the configuration, at the bitnet simulation
Of the imminent manifestation planned for me by the memory core;
I saw the horrid, pallid features of the craven, driven creature,
Of that rhymster over-reacher resurrected from before—
I saw his haunted features and the look of madness that he bore:
                      "Not that!" I pleaded, "nevermore!"

But the program, never veering, kept revising and repairing
Until I saw his visage peering red-eyed with its gimlet gore—
"I do not want this verbal horror! I do not want to mourn Lenore or
Ulalume, or spend my furor in this rhyming, pounding roar!
Re-program me!" I cried—demanded!—and fainted against the cubicle door
                      When the cursor spelled out *"Nevermore!"*

                      * * *

And now I've lived through three more missions, felt my atoms twist and fission,
Found myself in this position, huddled over a computer core—
Three times I've found myself a craven coward seeking for a haven,

Surcease from that metric Raven that pounds within me o'er and
    o'er—
From this ranting, chanting versing, from this meter I abhor:
                                  Quoth the program: "Nevermore."

So I wear his black mustaches; so I dream that I may slash his
Image…pray that I can crash this program's jingling, jangling
    core—
So I sit with fingers curling on the keyboard, data swirling,
All my energies unfurling to make me as I was before.
Done! Press *Enter!* That should do it! Make me as I was before!
                                  But the screen gloats, "Nevermore."

                                          —Michael R. Collings
                        Parody of Edgar Allen Poe, "The Raven"

BECAUSE I WOULD NOT STOP FOR DEATH

                                                          For Emily

> "The long sleeps of somec are only useful to those who are bored, who hope that by skipping over time they will live long enough to see something new"—Orson Scott Card, *Capitol*

Because I would not stop for Death,
Death tried to stop for me;
She placed her hand upon the land—
She touched the fevered sea.

She harvested vast fields of souls—
She struck this Earth with blight;
I hurried past the blasted stalks—
I tuned my fear to flight.

She tried to hold me back; she offered

Entropy and calm—
She curved her hands to scimitar blades,
She touched my nerveless palms.

I fled to paths between dark stars,
To curves that bisect space—
She followed me, the Lady Death,
And strove to win the race.

In tandem, Death and I pursued
Spin-wheeling galaxies;
We raced at light's velocity—
We took what we might seize

Of time and space and curvature—
We passed the speed of light
And entered a new Universe
Of Death—of Me—of Night.

And still we raved with frantic pace—
Attenuated life—
We passed all bounds of consciousness—
Became our mindless strife…

Mere moments have passed—and æons died—
Since I've begun to see
My Death and I are lock-embraced
Toward Infinity.

Pastiche on Emily Dickinson,
"Because I Could Not Stop for Death"

MY LAST NEMESIS

There he stands, looking as if alive
glowering down, baleful eyes and
scimitar smile. I have hung him

in my study to remind me,
to remind me always of my
danger—and of yours, my child. So
long now he has hunted me, as
if he did not understand my
gift of immortality. I keep him
there, gilt-framed and painted by my
own hand—eternal life has its
rewards, you know.
                       Who *is* that,
you ask? My foolish, foolish child!
There stands the mortal enemy,
Von Helsing in the flesh (or rather,
in the oils,). My nemesis and yours.
                       Speak up!
What's that? He's long-years dead, you say?
I don't believe it....
                       A century? More?
Then that's the reason I've not seen him
poking after shadows, strewing
magic wafers in my sleeping earth.
                       Ah well!
There he stands, corpse-still in oils,
nemesis, murderer, secret stalker
in the day. Mark him well, my
child, shun....
                       Of course I heard!
Yes! He's dead. And I'm not senile
yet, nor ever am to be. But listen
well, my child. I've lived long-years myself,
and well I know, my foolish child,
their searching, killing, prying kind
is just as lasting as our own.

There's ALWAYS *a Von Helsing!*

Pastiche on Robert Browning,
"My Last Duchess"

THE STREAM I TOOK

Two streams split in a green plain,
With no time to fish up both
And carry one rod, I stood in the rain
And followed ond down with eyes that strain
To find Walter, the fish of infinite growth;

Then waded down the other, just as clear,
And definitely showing a better prize,
Because of the enormous bank coming near;
So I crept up close, so Walter could not hear
Hoping he would fall victim to one of my flies;

Now both streams appeared the same
For each could easily bring a good catch.
But, the first would be left for someone else's game!
Knowing that this fish, Walter's his name,
Would end the day with a hell of a match.

I tell this now with heartfelt rue
For once on a cold and rainy day:
Two streams stood before me and I, on cue,
I took the one Walter travelled through,
And that choice took me up the river all the way.

Pastiche on Robert Frost,
"The Road Not Taken"

COMPRESSION III—LINKING VERBS

There is nothing wrong with *is*—or with any of its variants, *are, am, was, were, be, being, been*—or with other verbs designed primarily to simply connect a noun with another noun or an adverb—*seems, becomes, appears.*

Nothing at all.

Such verbs have formed an integral part of English for well over a millennium, in several instances remaining almost unchanged in form and function. Since English vocabulary and grammar have discarded a large number of similar elements over the same thousand years while these have endured, they obviously fulfill crucial roles.

Yet the fact remains that such verbs contribute frequently to bulky, padded, flat, uninteresting, often pretentious, and only rarely active or image-forming lines. In essence, they abrogate the fundamental nature of verbs and, instead of connecting two "things"—two nouns or noun substitutes—by detailing what one does to the other, they establish little more than an equation: A = B. An identity. A statement often bordering on the redundant. As with all such statements, whether mathematical or linguistic, the equation reverses easily: B = A. Logic demands that both statements identify the same truth, albeit in opposite order. Essentially, however, nothing happens or indeed can happen in such statements.

The trouble—for poetry at least—begins when such a verb links one or, more frequently, two abstractions, as in this distinctly non-poetic statement: "The decision of the administration was the reduction of salaries." Never mind that the statement defines an illogicality; a "decision" does not equate to a "reduction" but rather "to reduce." Or that 60% of the statement forms essentially blubber—fat: *the, of,* and *was* stringing together the highly abstract, non-visual, non-image-forming *decision, administration, reduction,* and *salaries.*

Most poets might automatically avoid such an obviously pedestrian sentence, or at the least break it into lines to disguise its flatness. A more alert poet might recognize, however, that performing several compression techniques might transform even this into a line or lines capable of strength and power.

The process follows these general stages:

First, identify the action. Grammatically, action centers in verbs, which in this case makes *is* the key word, yet it provides no sense of movement. But clearly something has happened here, with the word identifying that action hidden in the text. A moment's through provides the answer. Someone "decided" something. Transferring the verbal action into an abstract noun preceding *is* provides a valuable service for official spokespersons in our obsessively abstracted, distanced society: no one has to take credit—or, more crucially, bear blame—for an action. Instead, far more neutrally, a "decision *was* made."

Next, position the action word as the verb of the sentence. In this case, someone decided something.

Then, rearrange the remaining key words—the nouns—into subject and predicates, agents and acted upon: "The administration decided on a reduction of salaries." Return to the first step and identify the new action that has just emerged: *reduction* disguises a much stronger verb: *reduce*.

Again, rearrange the remaining key words: "The administration reduced salaries." If nothing else, we have compressed the statement from ten words to four—a loss of a full 60% of the original, including most of the function words or structure words. And we have a clear sense of an action.

Almost.

The next stage often presents the most difficulties: Focus action on a person or persons. An administration does not determine salary levels; an administration runs a corporate entity, a business, a school. Ultimately only a small portion of that larger group has the power to determine salaries. Identify as closely as possible where responsibility lies: "The president reduced salaries."

Not a particularly poetic line, perhaps, but with additional concentration on specific, action-filled words, we might end up with: "The president cut salaries" or "The president slashed wages."

See how far we have gone, from "The decision of the administration was the reduction of salaries" to "The president slashed wages." Notice also that the new sentence communicates not only

THE ART AND CRAFT OF POETRY, BY MICHAEL R. COLLINGS * 171

actor/acted-upon but does so with an obvious judgmental or evaluative tone.

How might this work in poetry?

The familiar opening lines of Eugene Fields' "'Little Boy Blue" depend heavily on forms of 'is':

> The little toy dog **is** covered with dust,
> But sturdy and staunch he stands;
> And the little toy soldier **is** red with rust,
> And his musket moulds in his hands.
> Time **was** when the little toy dog **was** new,
> And the soldier **was** passing fair;
> And that **was** the time when our Little Boy Blue
> Kissed them and put them there.

Ten verbs support the statements: *is, stands, is, moulds, was, was, was, was, kissed,* and *put*; only four define specific actions.

Now, being entirely unfair to Fields (who after all wrote for another time, to another audience, and from another poetics), what would happen if we revised the poem to emphasize action? The lines might now read:

> Dusty, the toy dog
> Stands, staunch and sturdy.
> Rusty, the musket
> Moulds in the toy soldier's hands.
>
> Once—a new stuffed dog,
> Once—a soldier passing fair;
> Kissed…then placed
> On a child's nursery shelf.

Thirty-six words as opposed to 61—just over half as many as in the original. Admittedly my revision has lost much of the poetry of Fields' verse, particularly in rhythm, rhyme, and music. Yet I would nonetheless argue that removing 'is' and 'was' and highlighting 'stands,' 'moulds,' 'kissed,' and 'placed' creates from the lines a more modern, more immediately accessible poetic experience.

The opening line of Part III asserted: "There is nothing wrong with *is*." This sentence and Fields' stanza considered above break no rules, fracture no grammatical conventions. In fact, in many cases, *is* or its variants may fill a useful purpose. Certain ideas fit more securely into poems as passive sentences. The following stanza,

> That winter,
> Snow began in January and fell for weeks.
> The road to Burlington **was** graded once a day,
> But we small pupils scuttled between iced
> Prison walls that towered two feet
> Over us as we threaded our long three miles
> To the school…,

emphasizes the snow, the road, the pupils struggling toward school. In this context, the identity of those who grade the road sinks to a low level of priority—particularly since the children would probably have no way of knowing who performed that crucial service; instead the fact of the grading surfaces…in a legitimately passive structure that accommodates meaning and tone within the stanza.

Similarly, in the final lines of "The Lost Islander," a shaped poem written by one of my former students at Pepperdine,

> my flower crown has withered,
> my sharp brow has sagged,
> the grass is prickling my chest,
> the dance fires are soot and ash,
> the tight-skin drums lie still, alone.
> i stare stolid at the wavering horizon,
> i'm still waiting for the trees.
> i'm still waiting for the trees,

careful placement of *is, are,* and *am* in its contracted form, along with the auxiliary *has*, emphasizes the loneliness, the tremendous age, and the ultimate passivity of the Easter Island monoliths, as does the fact that neither of the true verbs—*lie* or *stare*—implies movement even as each defines an act. Nothing happens to the monoliths, nothing can.

In the end, then, "there is nothing wrong with *is*," when poets chose it or words like it consciously, with an eye and an ear for its potentials as well as an awareness of its abuses.

[By the way, except for in the first sentence and its repetition throughout Part III, *is* does not appear as a sentence verb; it occurs only as a word-used-as-a-word, an entity, to complete the implied phrase "the word *is*."]

20. REVISION [III]

Completely revise any poem written from these exercises, using the questions below. The new version *must* re-conceive the original, casting it into an entirely different form (e.g., free-verse into metrical, free-form into stanzaic, non-rhyming into rhyming). Length: minimum of 20 lines

1. Do line lengths and typography function purposefully and effectively? Are lines shaped and formed, or do they just occur? How do lines relate to content? Do any lines draw attention to themselves rather than to the poem as a whole

2. How does the poem create its music—evaluate the effectiveness of alliteration, assonance, consonance; rhyme, both internal and end-stopped; subtle versus overt patterns. How do these devices relate to tone, atmosphere, feeling?

3. How does the poem create its rhythms: Does the poem incorporate stress, meter, typography, syntactical patterns, syllabics, or breath units?

4. How successfully has the poem compressed language to express meaning? Could it be further compressed? Are there any unnecessary words? What is the poem's subject? How do the poem's images relate to content? Is there a difference between the physical object[s] about which the poem speaks and its true subject[s]? Is the poem intended to be metaphorical? What is the tenor? The vehicle?

5. Is the final version stronger than the original? How and why? Do the revisions increase the sense of "sophisticated" over "simple"? Does the final version have a more universal appeal than the original, speaking to readers without your private complex of memories, emotions, and understanding?

6. Has revising the poem helped you grow? Is it *true* in the deepest sense of the word? Has revising it expanded your perceptions of your self, your art, and your world?

10,000,000,000,000,000,000,000,000,000,000 [Original]
  years from now, when the final proton
  sighs and dies into black nothingness, when
    [*"the executioner's sword descending with languid grace"**]
  only electron and positron survive
  of all the forms the Big Bang gave

  form to, when attenuated particles managed
  by magnetic fields and foraging

  through infinity spare lightyears distant
  from each other agree with full consent
            [*"'vaster than empires, and more slow'"**]
  to constitute an Entity,
  when time and space slow to full eternity…,
  …,

  Entity—galactic-huge, sentient inorganic
  thought incapable of peace or panic
              [*"wispy magnetic consorts"* *]
  decides (over a century of archaic years)
  to move a spiral arm through ghosts of stars,

  sweep meditatively across remnant-memories
  of chemistry and physics and cosmology,

  disturb its subatomic particles a fraction
  of a parsec, and with that inarticulated action,
        [*"to the slow thumping of the universal heart"* *]
  move appendage a minimal, millennial nod,
  and contemplates imagining a god.

—Michael R. Collings quoting
Gregory Benford's "Introduction" to
Far Futures (1995). In *The Leading Edge*, 1996.

CREATION: ON CONSIDERING THE IMPONDERABLE MATTER OF THE UNIVERSE [Revision]

unmade protons sigh//transform   translated
electrons/positrons   attenuated
particles managed by magnetic fields
forage through infinity   counsel   yield
consent to constitute each Entity,
time and space slow to full eternity…,

ENTITY   galactic-huge organic
thought unable yet of peace or panic
sweeps meditative prescient-memories
to chemistry   physics   cosmology
twists subatomic particles their fraction
with each inarticulated action

moves INTELLIGENCES a millennial nod
and contemplates imagining its GODS

—Michael R. Collings
Elemental Sonets, 1999.

PEANUT AND THE CRAB PATROL

Trade winds still
As darkness fades;
Buzzing, flitting sand flies
Gather like clouds on rainy days.
Horned oxen stand motionless
On marl roads,

Ribbed and hung.

White Egrets perch on honches,
Like blazing angels,
Silent, still.
Beams break corners in sudden
Exposure, and whining

Gears grow louder;
Egrets alight in noiseless,
Regal flight, and swarms
Disperse like blackness.
Peanut's rusted plantation truck
Pulls up,

Covered with boys and
Lantern lights, outlining native
Faces and set, still features; pursed,
Determined, excited. Barbed staffs
Adorn their hands like Vetu warriors—
Silent Vetu warriors.

Slight-figured Peanut leads
On foot past stubborn, sleepy, road-
Side beasts and deep brown pools
Of marshy waste. Lantern shadows
Eye red glowing eyes, Caimon
Aligators, or are they green salamanders?

The Crab Patrol stops short. Peanut
Disappears past jungle vines and
Strewn Grapetree leaves—but
Not one sound; all silent, still.
Only lantern flickers on
Excited, wary faces, straining...

Into the blackness beyond,
With its duppies, ironshore ogres, frights
And voodoo vibes, strange lights, poisonous bites,

Wire-haired, snorting boars and anaconda prey.
Beckoning jungle with its innocent veil
of sweet-smelling vines and flowers.

A blood-curdling scream rips through the veil!
Seven bursting lungs of pent-up fright break
Forest peace, all at once, crashing lights blow out like night—
The Crab Patrol rushes past, leaving slight-figured
Peanut grinning and holding a spiny-clawed crab.

PEANUT AND THE CRAB PATROL [original]

would scour the humid night
with flashlights   poking extra-
terrestrial beams   unearthing Red
Stripe beer bottles   old rusty hooks,
Prince Albert sardine cans lying
stagnant under Grapetree leaves

a rustle!

scurrying lights and excited whispers

ssssh!

cupid ears move forward on tip-toes

cr
  u
    n
      c
        h!

shadows leap   stumble   yell
disco night   loud screams of fright
flashlights crash and still

>   hung heads turn back

This poem has undergone several transformations, both in form and in content. Which of the three works most effectively to communicate subject, tone/atmosphere, image, and theme:

AFRICAN VIOLETS [original]

>   Mabel Grafel, old-maid school-marm and
>   Terror of the fifth grade rowdies,
>   Kept rows of violets in rigid formations on
>
>   A long, brown, institutional table tucked—
>   A lonely afterthought—beneath the
>   Window-banks along the north-most wall of
>
>   Burlington School. That winter, snow
>   Began in January and fell for weeks.
>   The road to Burlington was graded once a day,
>
>   But we small pupils scuttled between iced
>   Prison walls that towered two feet
>   Over us as we threaded our long three miles
>
>   To the school. Everything froze. Headbolt heaters
>   Froze while still plugged into engines;
>   Sewer lines burst, turning whole long blocks of new
>
>   Backyards into only slightly fragrant skating rinks—
>   We ran P.E. races on ice-slick sidewalks,
>   Tucked inside thick fur-lined parkas, and still
>
>   Half-freezing lips and noses with each painful breath.
>   But in *her* room, in rigid forms laid out upon the
>   Tabletop, her violets prismed winters into spring.

MABEL GRAFEL [revision 1]

Mabel Grafel—unsmiling, iron-haired,
Grim gargoyle to all fifth-grade rowdies—
Kept rows of violets in neat formations on
A narrow table tucked as if
A lonely afterthought beneath high
Window-banks along the north-most wall of
Burlington School.
                    That winter,
Snow began in January and fell for weeks.
The road to Burlington was graded once a day,
But we small pupils scuttled between iced
Prison walls that towered two feet
Over us as we threaded our long three miles
To the school.
                    Everything froze.
Headbolt heaters froze while still
Plugged into engines; sewer lines burst,
Turning whole long blocks of new backyards
Into only slightly fragrant skating rinks—
We ran short PhysEd races on ice-slick walks,
Tucked inside thick fur-lined parkas, and still
Half-froze our lips and noses with each painful
Breath.
            But in *her* room, laid out
In rigid rows upon brown boards that glowed
Rich birch-grain-gold in the angled light,
Her violets prismed winter into spring.

AFRICAN VIOLETS [revision 2]

Mabel Grafel, oldmaid schoolmarm, terror
of fifthgrade rowdies, preened rows of violets
in frigid formations on brown-veneered
tables tucked by the warmer, brighter, west-
most wall at Burlington School. That winter,
snow began in January, fell all

month. Snowplows scraped roads clean once a day. Her
pupils scuttled between iced prisonwalls
on our long treks to school. Hot-oil headbolt
heaters froze in engines; sewer lines burst;
we ran PhysEd on ice-slick sidewalks, tucked
in fur-lined parkas, freezing with each breath.
But in *her* room, rigid tabletop rings
of violets prismed winter into spring.

PERSONAL POETRY INVENTORY

1. Three reasons why I write

2. Three reasons why I write poetry [as opposed to other worthwhile genres]

3. Three purposes I want my poetry to achieve

4. Three strategies I use to achieve those purposes

5. Three devices/structures/techniques I find particularly useful in my poetry

6. Reasons why those specific devices/structures/techniques are important in my poetry

7. Three devices/structures/techniques I rarely use in my poetry

8. Reasons why I choose not to use those devices, structures, or techniques

9. Three ways I know when a poem is finished

10. I consider myself a
    - FORMALIST, i.e., I frequently use traditional forms and structures, including
        - Rhyme as a primary musical device
        - Meter as a primary rhythmic device
        - Stanzas of pre-determined line count
        - Relatively regular line-lengths
        - Sonnets
        - Quatrains and/or Triplets
        - Ballads
        - Other
    - SYLLABIC POET, i.e., I frequently use forms based primarily on syllable count, including
        - Stanzaic syllabics
        - 'Nonce' syllabics
        - Haiku
        - Tanka
        - Cinquain
        - Other
    - OPEN-FORM POET, i.e., I consider myself primarily a 'free verse' poem, creating my own fundamental forms but using such structures and devices as
        - Controlled but varying line length
        - Repeated syntactical structures, such as anaphors (repetition of an initial word or phrase over several

lines)
- ❑ Breath units as a primary means of determining line length
- ❑ Non-metrical stresses as a primary means of line length

11. I frequently and consciously use the following in my poetry:
    - ❑ Simple sense IMAGERY, usually visual
    - ❑ More complex IMAGERY that attempts to elicit several sensory responses simultaneously
    - ❑ SIMILES, primarily to convey sense impressions
    - ❑ SIMILES, primarily to convey more complex responses than simple sense impressions
    - ❑ METAPHORS, in which the poem spells out the relationship between both the TENOR (the abstract thing or idea I wish to talk about) and the VEHICLE (the concrete thing or idea to which I compare the abstraction)
    - ❑ METAPHORS, in which the TENOR is implicit or assumed, while the poem appears to focus exclusively on the vehicle
    - ❑ SYMBOLS within my poems
    - ❑ More complex SYMBOLS, in which the principle theme or ideas of the poem—considering individual poem as an integral whole—is communicated indirectly, through the mediation of the poems

12. I frequently and consciously use the following sound devices in creating the music of my poetry:
    - ❑ Alliteration
    - ❑ Assonance
    - ❑ Consonance
    - ❑ Full Rhyme
    - ❑ Slant-, Skewed-, Half-Rhyme
    - ❑ Others

13. In general, I am
    - ☐ Satisfied with the directions and expertise my poems demonstrate
    - ☐ Satisfied, but am eager to expand into new modes and explore new means of creating art
    - ☐ Frequently unsatisfied with the level of my poetry, especially in terms of
        - ☐ My use of language
        - ☐ My understanding of structure
        - ☐ The limits I impose—consciously or unconsciously—on my Imagination
        - ☐ The limits I impose—consciously or unconsciously—on my Ideas
        - ☐ My technical and mechanical Proficiency
        - ☐ Other
    - ☐ Deeply dissatisfied with the level of my poetry
    - ☐ About to give up on writing poetry at all

ABOUT THE AUTHOR

MICHAEL R. COLLINGS is an Emeritus Professor of English at Seaver College, Pepperdine University, where he directed the Creative Writing Program for over two decades. He has published multiple volumes of poetry, novels, short fiction, and scholarly studies of such contemporary writers as Stephen King, Dean R. Koontz, and Orson Scott Card. He is now retired and lives in his native state of Idaho.

www.ingramcontent.com/pod-product-compliance
Lightning Source LLC
Chambersburg PA
CBHW030932090426
42737CB00007B/394